WAKE UP, AMERICA!

UNDERSTAND THE US CONSTITUTION

AND

GET INVOLVED

BY

FRANK ELLIOTT SISSON II

ISBN: 1478260289
ISBN-13: 9781478260288
Library of Congress Control Number: 2012912950
CreateSpace, North Charleston, South Carolina

To my
wife, children, grandchildren,
and those who follow

TABLE OF CONTENTS

PROLOGUE

A power struggle is currently taking place between the Federal Government and the governments of the fifty states. The founders of our country envisioned a Federal Government with limited powers, as defined in the Constitution. Today the Federal Government is gaining power while state governments are losing power. If this trend continues, it will be to our detriment. We all need to understand the Constitution in order to take appropriate action to reverse the course of this power struggle.

INTRODUCTION

I am a West Point graduate and Air Force pilot, retiring after twenty years of service to the country. While in the service, I earned master's degrees in both aeronautical engineering and management and following those graduate programs, I worked in aircraft acquisition programs in the government's program offices. I also spent a few years as a director of an engineering organization that modified Air Force aircraft into high performance airborne research laboratories. These aircraft performed basic research missions all over the world doing studies such as weather, gravity, nuclear explosion detection, and solar eclipses. These studies occurred in the 1950's, prior to our going into space, but were advanced airborne research at the time. I also flew aerial combat missions in Korea and Vietnam.

Following military service, I joined the civilian business arena and worked in marketing products to the aircraft industry. I also spent a few years in the aviation export business and traveled all over the world offering US products to foreign buyers. I left that business to become a consultant to the US Defense Department and conducted technical studies in support of the military services and lived in the Washington, DC area. Following that, I moved to Wichita, Kansas, and worked for an aircraft manufacturer for a couple of years and then founded my own company which was marketing products to the local aircraft industry representing manufacturers from all over the world. In 2005, after seventeen years, I sold the business and have been retired ever since. Following retirement, I found the time to sit back and do some writing. My first book, A Ransomed Yankee, took nearly three years to research and write. It is a unique Civil War naval story about my great grandfather, Captain of the whale ship, Milo, who was ransomed by the Confederate cruiser Shenandoah in the Bering Sea, to take prisoners aboard from six destroyed whalers on June 23, 1865; it also covers the last shot fired in the war on June 28, by the Shenandoah, and that occurred in the Bering Strait, near the Arctic Ocean, where nine more whale ships were destroyed

A few years ago, I became interested in the US Constitution and decided to purchase five small leather books, very nicely bound, and sent one to each of my grown children and kept one for myself. I kept my copy on my computer desk and began to use it whenever an issue arose regarding the Constitution. It is surprising how often this happens, and I found myself using the little book frequently as issues arose often. Then I made the effort to read through the book and try to memorize all of its contents. Then I went further, I rewrote the Constitution in my own words and thought this would help strengthen my knowledge of the document. It did do that and I began to understand the wording more and more. Then, to make a long story short, I began to do a lot of research on the Internet into the issues that influenced the writing of the Constitution. I read old books written by famous authors including Robert Filmer, Thomas Hobbes, John Locke, Thomas Paine, the Federalist papers, and publications from those who were there debating the issues. I really began to grasp the meaning of the Constitution and the role it plays in the direction of our country. It is the most important document we have and it needs to be understood by all of us so we can take action to protect our way of life and our freedom. In 2011, I decided to write a book about the Constitution so that it would help explain why it was written, who was involved, when it was ratified, how amendments were processed, and where we stand with the document today.

This is a book about the state of our country in terms of reflecting the goals of our US Constitution by our founders. By reading publications printed at the time of the writing of the Constitution, one can draw conclusions about the principal leaders involved in its development and what their intentions were for managing the document. We need to know what they thought about managing the Constitution to reflect changing conditions as the world changes. It turns out that the founders fully expected that the document would be changed to reflect changing conditions. In fact, they actually rushed through the final push to get the Constitution ratified in order to at least have an official document from which to move forward and to make amendments later on. Apparently, some people believe that the document should never change as the wording will last forever. However that is not to say the founders believed that; they knew that changes, or amendments, would be necessary and that is why they included

Article V which provides for amending the Constitution. What is important is to know that the founders anticipated amendments and that they were not only comfortable with that issue but also felt it was necessary to have that written into the Constitution. They also were wise to offer two methods of approving proposed amendments and two ways to ratify those proposals that are officially approved. The Congress or the States may approve proposals, but only the States may ratify; the President is out of the loop on this issue.

As the United States of America is now more than two hundred years old, it's time to take a close look at how our country has evolved up until now and try to make sense of it. To do this we will start before the beginning of written history and try to piece together the steps taken that have led to where we are today. Doing this may help explain the current state of our nation and highlight issues that may have come between us and a more perfect government, as was described by our founders. More importantly, we may learn how we as citizens of this great nation can insist on bringing about changes to our Constitution that will guarantee our freedom, property, and happiness, as our founders sought for all of us.

THE EVOLUTION OF GOVERNMENTS

To help you understand where we are today, the following pages provide a brief review of history learned from both intuitive reasoning as well as written literature that dates all the way back to the beginning of written history and before. This review will skip over many events in history in an attempt to provide a simple overview of some major events that have taken place. In this way we will have some perspective on how we, as a country, have arrived where we are today.

No one knows for certain how governments came into being and when that movement began. This phenomenon occurred long before mankind could write and communicate; history was passed down through stories from father to son and so on. Numerous writers, such as Machiavelli, Thomas Hobbes, Robert Filmer, John Locke, and Thomas Paine, among other well-known philosophers and historians, wrote about individuals and their natural environments and individual rights. All philosophers, however, generally agree that all humans are born with certain natural and unalienable rights and that each person has the right to protect himself or herself from all who would do them harm.

In the early days of civilization, people had no governments, and each individual was on his or her own to survive by whatever means he or she could amass. There were no laws, no regulations, no guidance, nor any way to know what was right or wrong. Consequently heads of families were inclined to take whatever action they could to protect their families and survive. These were not easy times for humanity, as people were constantly on guard and being pursued by others for the property they had obtained through their own labor. Furthermore, people discovered that certain tasks took more than one individual to accomplish, and therefore they would, no doubt, ask friends or acquaintances for help when needed and returned the favor when their services were needed. So it would be a foregone conclusion that, in this way, communities were formed naturally and people in communities probably got along fairly well together.

It is probably safe to say that the original heads of government were the male heads of families. They were for all intents and purposes the first monarchs, and each head of a family established the rules and regulations for his family, mainly to safeguard each family member and to provide a defense against anyone wanting to harm a member or steal property from the family. This theory follows the natural law of all living creatures, in which nature provides protection of the young by the parents until the young can fend for themselves. Humankind and all animals were simply following the rules of nature, as it was the natural thing to do. To help explain the unknown, humans created many different religions over time to answer their questions about where we came from and why we are here. These thoughts subsequently evolved into numerous gods that looked over humanity and provided acceptable answers to tough questions.

The concept of families as individual monarchies worked so well that soon families realized that if they banded together as one community, all families would have a better chance of improving conditions within the community by working together on joint projects as well as protecting one another from outside harm. So, more than likely, they got together and each family agreed regarding how they would elect a leader to act on their behalf for the protection of property and the security and happiness for all. Each head of a family had input as to who would lead the community, as well as the rules they would all use in their everyday lives to build the community, safeguard property, protect lives, and promote happiness.

It is also assumed that those who became leaders did so based on a natural majority vote. This was likely done by the initiative of the families, and the outcome was that the leader represented and worked for the families within that particular community. The families were the so-called owners, and the leader was the executive who provided the services. In general the outcome of these relationships was that community projects were built, security was greatly improved, private property was protected, and happiness among families was enhanced.

In a sense the communities that resulted from these beginnings became tribes. These tribes grew and grew and became powerful communities that set the trend of things to come. The people within each tribe were the de facto owners of the tribe, in that they all agreed to become part of the tribe and to elect in some way the leaders who would serve all of the tribe's members. What happened could have been predicted; some leaders were good and some were bad. The good ones served the people; the bad ones became tyrants and enslaved the people. This phenomenon has repeated itself ever since.

As the centuries passed, the population of the world increased, and the size of tribes increased and became large enough to become sovereign states and nations. We can learn much about the early times of civilization from ancient and other religious documents, and certainly the Bible. Over the years, religious scholars, philosophers, and students of ancient history have studied these writings, and these documents tell us a great deal about how people lived and how nations were governed. The Old Testament tells the story of life in the early years of modern civilization and of kings and monarchs who governed and fought wars and were either benevolent or tyrannical rulers.

Kings, monarchs, or dictators ruled the early nations. These nations included freemen and slaves. Slaves had no say in anything and were generally acquired as prizes from nations that lost wars in battle. Freemen, however, were at the mercy of the monarch. If they were lucky, they had a benevolent monarch; if they weren't they had a tyrannical despot as their leader. Generally people did not like having a king or monarch, as they were never really free and independent, and that is the natural state humans have always wanted.

Ancient Greece was perhaps the first major nation to establish a democratic type of government in which the people elected their officials. This was a difficult democracy to manage, as all people voted on all proposals. Over time this process became cumbersome, which ultimately led to the collapse of the Greek government. Greece spawned Alexander the Great, who became a famous military general and almost conquered the world between the years after his father, the King, was assassinated in 336 BC to Alexander's death. Alexander was only thirty-three years old when he died mysteriously in 323 BC, after he already had taken control over much of the Eastern world, but the leaders who followed him could not govern the massive size of the expanded country; thus, Greece slowly fell into ruin. Around two thousand years ago, the Romans followed with another democratic-type government that seemed to follow in the footsteps of Alexander. They conquered most of Europe, northern Africa, and the Middle East. The Roman government, however, was more of a republican form of government in which representatives of the people voted on laws and regulations that governed the empire. Julius Caesar was the principal leader and military general during the Roman glory days, but he was assassinated and followed by weaker leaders who became monarchs, until finally Rome fell from grace a few centuries following the death of Caesar in 44 BC.

By this time the world was becoming wiser and more sophisticated. In the centuries that followed the crucifixion of Jesus Christ and the establishment of Christianity, Europe evolved into a number of sovereign states, including France, Germany, Italy, Holland, Spain, Portugal, Scandinavia, Poland, Russia, and England. Christianity had spread and was the main religion practiced across the Western world. France and England entered into battles to establish a monarch numerous times through the first ten or so centuries following the birth of Christ. In all cases it's safe to say that the people were divided into two classes, the rich and the poor. The rich were the royals who were loyal to the monarch and were provided with wealth and property in exchange for their loyal service during both peace and war. The rich were few in number while the poor were many.

In England the poor had very little to say about political or governmental matters, but they still had enough power to finally force the English monarchy to pass a people's constitution that gave certain rights to all English citizens. This was called the Magna Carta and became law in the year 1055. In 1492 another event took place that changed the world forever— Christopher Columbus's discovery of America. The explorer was seeking a route to the Far East to search for the treasures of the Orient, but instead he found the continent of America. Following that discovery the world began to change dramatically.

THE AMERICAN COLONIES

Colonial America under British rule started with a whimper with the arrival of the first settlers in Jamestown, Virginia, in 1607. They began the journey with the knowledge that Columbus had discovered this great body of land. In June of 1606, King James I granted a charter to the Virginia Company, a group of London entrepreneurs, to establish a satellite English settlement in the Chesapeake region of North America. In December of that year, 104 settlers sailed from London with instructions to settle Virginia, find gold, and seek a water route to the Orient. Recent historical and archaeological research at the site of Jamestown suggests that many of the artisans, craftsmen, and laborers who accompanied them made every effort to make the colony succeed with little help from King James I.

A few years later, in 1620, the *Mayflower* arrived to settle Plymouth with people who wanted to begin a new life to practice their religion freely and independently. They were called the Pilgrims. Both the Jamestown and Plymouth colonists had their work cut out for them. They had to fend for themselves—withstanding violent weather, finding and building shelter, hunting for and growing food, caring for their families and children, and fighting Native Americans. It was a tough life, but the settlers were up to the task and ultimately succeeded in both colonies. Early on, England didn't interfere with the everyday issues of colonial government; this was left up to the colonies themselves, and the settlers were pleased with their relative freedom.

For the next hundred years or so, the colonies expanded in population as immigrants arrived from England and Europe. Colonial towns and cities grew in size during this period. There were, however, continual battles with the Native Americans, including King Philip's War (also known as the First Indian War) in the 1670s, which lasted several years and cost many lives, but the colonists prevailed. Despite these hardships, the colonies became economically self-sufficient and made great social and educational accomplishments. They produced their food through the relatively efficient farming of plants and the raising of animals. They even exported surplus products of food and local products to foreign markets. These products included fish, whale oil, furs, and lumber, among other goods. As the economy thrived over time, King George III became more interested in taking advantage of opportunities to control the export business and to increase English revenues by collecting tariffs and taxes, which didn't go over very well with the colonists. By the mid-eighteenth century, the colonies had increased from the original two to thirteen sepa-rate colonial states, and they were beginning to rebel.

In the late sixteenth century, the upper class and the enlight-ened thinkers in England greatly respected the works of Thomas Hobbes, an English philosopher and writer. At that time England was going through numerous battles to settle on a king who would be acceptable to all of the people. Hobbes wrote that because adults are "equal" in the capacity to threaten one another's lives, there is no natural source of authority to dictate how individuals should live and conduct their lives. He strongly opposed arguments that established that monarchs have a natural or God-given right to rule over others. Yet, in his life, Hobbes was associated with the class of people who were in the same league with the king. Even so, he strongly advocated for a better form of government than a monarchy. His ideas influenced widely read philosophers who followed him, including England's John Locke and the American colonies' Thomas Paine, both of whom sought a form of government in which the leader was temporary in his term and certainly not a hereditary monarch.

In the mid-1600s, English philosopher Robert Filmer wrote in his book, *Patriarcha and Other Writings,* that God had ordained Adam as the original monarch and that all eldest sons in Adam's line of descendants inherited the monarchy for all mankind. John Locke greatly disputed this theory after the publication of Filmer's book. Locke said there was no way to prove such a theory and certainly no way to trace Adam's line forward. The point here is that people were thinking about the origin of monarchies at that time, and they were disturbed by the power of the monarch, or in the case of England, the king. Filmer was trying to rationalize where the monarchs came from; however, his argument was full of holes. Locke took this opportunity to write about natural laws and the rights of all people to be free and independent. His book *Second Treatise of Government* was widely read in England and in the American colonies, and greatly influenced Thomas Paine, who wrote *Common Sense*, the publication that probably had the greatest influence on the Declaration of Independence. *Common Sense* was essentially a written rally point for the colonies to declare their independence from England, and Paine laid out all the reasons for doing just that.

In the meantime, British authority took on a harsher relationship with the colonies. Anger and rage continued to build among the colonists and culminated in the Boston Tea Party in 1773. This was an act of defiance on the part of the colonists to demonstrate against taxation without representation. The next year, between September 5 and October 26, 1774, the first Continental Congress was held in Carpenter's Hall in Philadelphia and consisted of fifty-six delegates from twelve of the thirteen colonial states that would become the United States of America. Georgia did not attend, as it needed British assistance with internal problems in the colony at that time. The delegates—who included George Washington, then a colonel of the Virginia volunteers; Patrick Henry; and John Adams—were elected by their respective colonial assemblies. The main outcome of the convention was that the delegates organized an economic boycott of Great Britain and petitioned the king for a redress of grievances. In late November 1774, King George III opened Parliament with a speech that condemned Massachusetts and the demands made by the colonies; things were not looking good between Great Britain and the colonies.

In the aftermath of King George's speech to Parliament, the Articles of Confederation were drafted in mid-1776, and an approved version was sent to each colonial state for ratification in late 1777. The formal ratification by all thirteen colonial states was completed in early 1781. Even when not yet ratified, this document provided domestic and international legitimacy for the Continental Congress to direct the American Revolutionary War, to conduct diplomacy with European nations, and to deal with territorial issues and Native-American relations. The Articles of Confederation became the de facto constitution of the United States of America and legitimized its government. The complete text of the Articles of Confederation appears in Appendix II.

The Revolutionary War actually began prior to the ratification of the Articles of Confederation, with the battles of Lexington and Concord taking place in April 1775. Following these battles, the colonies made several attempts toward reconciliation with England. King George, however, refused these attempts and declared that the colonies were in a state of open and avowed rebellion. In June 1775, Congress established the Continental Army and appointed George Washington commander in chief

In June 1776 a committee appointed by Congress asked Thomas Jefferson to write a draft of the Declaration of Independence to declare that the colonies had the right to—and should—be free and independent states. Congress debated the draft and passed it on July 4, 1776; from then on the colonies were changed forever. A complete version of the Declaration of Independence appears in Appendix I.

The official Revolutionary War followed soon after the passing of the Declaration of Independence, as King George did not accept the Declaration and demanded an immediate cessation of colonial independence. He rationalized that the British military was the most feared in the world and would soon subdue the colonies and bring them back in line under his realm. This, of course, did not happen, as the American rebels fought furious battles under General Washington with very little support from the Continental Congress in terms of funding and supplies. After the hostilities began, the colonies became states, and all of the states wrote and ratified sovereign state constitutions. In all cases the state constitutions supported strong legislatures and weak executives. The Continental Congress, however, had no executive or judicial branch and was incapable of providing sufficient support to the American army to fight the British. Despite this, the British finally surrendered, and the United States prevailed in a treaty signed on September 3, 1783. This document was officially called the Treaty of Paris. The weaknesses of the Continental Congress, however, were widely known and were addressed in the Constitutional Convention in 1787.

THE CONSTITUTIONAL CONVENTION

After the war, there was widespread support among the representatives sent to the Constitutional Convention for changes in the Articles of Confederation in order to correct its problems, primarily that there were no executive or judiciary branches in the Confedertion. The forthcoming convention, called the Constitutional Convention, was held in a room at the State House in Philadelphia between May and September 1787 and actually spawned the need for a completely different constitution. The resulting document was the Constitution of the United States of America, ratified by the consent of twelve of the thirteen colonial states on September 17, 1787.

The new constitution that evolved was created to join the sovereign states in a union that would offer certain benefits to all states by delegating specific powers to a federal overseer that would provide benefits and protection to the states that had joined the union. It was not the intent of the founders to create a single powerful nation under one single government.

These twelve states consisted of Georgia, Maryland, Massachusetts, New Hampshire, New Jersey, New York, North

Carolina, Pennsylvania, South Carolina, Connecticut, Delaware, and Virginia. Rhode Island was the last state to ratify the Constitution, which occurred on May 29, 1790, when the state was assured that the first ten amendments, the Bill of Rights, would be incorporated into the Constitution. As we know, the Constitution gave us three branches of government, the executive, legislative, and judiciary branches. It also made the government subservient to the people of the country through a representative form of government and term limits for elected officials. This information is the starting place for the analysis that follows in this book.

This book outlines the foregoing events and occurrences as a brief review of how government has evolved over the past several thousand years in order to provide a background of more modern events that have made the United States of America the nation it is today and how we can make it better. The purpose of this book, however, is to review how far we have come today under our Constitution, which was originally created for the American people by representatives from all the sovereign colonial states following the Declaration of Independence and the winning of the Revolutionary War. It took several years to debate the many issues of the day and write a Constitution that would be acceptable to all of the colonial states; consequently it was a long and difficult undertaking. All of the men involved in the debate were civic leaders in their own right, students of history, and well-read gentlemen, some of whom spoke several languages.

The principal leaders included Thomas Jefferson, James Madison, Alexander Hamilton, Benjamin Franklin, George Washington, and George Mason, among many others. A key issue was how much power the Federal Government should have. Some wanted a strong Federal Government while others wanted a limited Federal Government with more power to remain within each of the states. The final outcome was that the Federal Government was granted limited powers as enumerated in Article I, Section 8 of the ratified US Constitution.

Another great influence in the ongoing debates regarding what should be written into the Constitution were the Federalist Papers, which were published mainly by Alexander Hamilton, James Madison, and John Jay. These documents covered the major issues regarding the Constitution and provided information both pro and con for readers to digest. The Federalist Papers helped people across the country understand the issues and how the Constitution would affect everyone. The problem was—and has been all along—how to interpret the words in the Constitution as they are written; some are ambiguous, which has caused concern over the years regarding many political and governmental issues. The founders were aware of the Constitution's shortcomings, but to get the job done without further delay, they decided to go ahead with what they had; the ambiguities could be addressed later. This is why Article V was written the way it was; it allowed for the Constitution to be amended whenever there was a good reason. The founders didn't want an easy amendment process, but they did want to make it possible. Furthermore, many of the delegates wanted to incorporate a Bill of Rights into the Constitution in order to highlight and protect specific freedoms and assure that they would be a part of the Constitution. Again, in order to proceed without delay, the delegates agreed to wait until the

Constitution was ratified and then to amend the Constitution with the Bill of Rights soon thereafter.

After many lengthy debates, the Constitution finally was ratified by the majority of states needed for ratification on September 17, 1787. This event gave us a Federal Government that would ensure protection from foreign aggressors by appointing the president as commander in chief; by providing for a central authority to deal with foreign affairs; by providing for a central authority to deal with interstate commerce; and by providing for a central financial authority. All powers not enumerated for the Federal Government were retained by the states and the people. It was a great new approach to national government, which, for the first time. put the people as superior to the government in that the government was to serve the people and not the reverse. The ultimate result was that the United States of America became the first true land of the free and also the hope for mankind all over the world.

Also on September 17, 1787, a convention of the ten states that already had ratified the Constitution was held in New York City. The purpose was to officially set a procedure and date for electors from the several states to assemble and formally finalize the election of representatives, senators, and the president in order to make the outcome official and put the government in motion. This was accomplished by the convention and made official by the signature of George Washington, president of the convention. Around eighteen months later, on March 4, 1789, Congress met for the first time in Federal Hall in New York City to begin the new government under the Constitution. On

April 1 the House achieved a quorum and elected its leaders. On April 6 the Senate achieved a quorum and counted ballots from the state electors and announced that George Washington and John Adams were elected president and vice president respectively. George Washington was officially inaugurated as the first president of the United States of America on April 30, 1789, at Federal Hall in New York City. Following the inauguration, the United States began its journey to greatness. In 1790, Congress moved to Congress Hall in Philadelphia to conduct the business of government. One of the first orders of business for the new government was to amend the Constitution with the first ten amendments, also known as the Bill of Rights. Congress remained in Congress Hall, Philadelphia, until 1800, and during that year, moved the Congress to Washington, D.C.

The following chapter provides a brief overview of the Constitution in a condensed version. The complete text of the US Constitution appears in Appendix III.

A REVIEW OF THE RATIFIED CONSTITUTION

The following is a condenced version of the Constitution and not the actual text. I have written this version so the reader can gain a better understanding of the document in words that I have used so readers can quickly understand the document more clearly.

Preamble: We the people of the United States, in Order to form a more perfect Union, establish Justice, insure domestic Tranquility, provide for the common defence, promote the general Welfare and secure the Blessings of Liberty to ourselves and our Posterity, do ordain and establish this Constitution for the United States of America.

Our founders' goal: liberty for ourselves and our posterity.

Article I, Section 1: Establishes the legislative power of Congress, which shall consist of the Senate and the House of Representatives.

Congress is defined as the House of Representatives and the Senate.

Article I, Section 2: Defines the House and qualifications for becoming a representative.

A representative must be at least twenty-five years old and a citizen of the United States for at least seven years. Representatives shall be chosen every second year by the people of the states. The number of representatives from each state shall be according to the number of free persons, excluding Native Americans, who were not taxed and were considered three-fifths of all other persons. States determined the prerequisites for voting, and all states had their own rules. Some required that to vote one must either pay tax or have a guaranteed income of a certain amount. Some required ownership of property. Some made no disqualification for race or color; these were mostly Northern states. The Southern states had their own rules for voting.

Article I, Section 3: Defines the Senate and qualifications for becoming a senator.

A Senator must be at least thirty years old and a citizen of the United States for at least nine years. There will be two senators from each state, chosen by the legislature thereof, and the term for senator will be six years. One-third of the senators shall be chosen every two years. The rotation was established during the first six years of the union and is now in place. The Seventeenth Amendment, however, changed the election of senators from the state legislators to the people on April 8, 1913. This limited the influence of the states in Congress and gave more power to the political parties. This was not a good idea.

Article I, Section 4: Assigns to the states the times, places, and manner of holding elections for representatives and senators.

The times, places, and manner of holding elections for senators and representatives shall be prescribed in each state by the legislature thereof, but Congress may at any time by law make or alter such regulations, except as to the places of choosing senators.

The Congress must assemble at least once each year, and each meeting shall be on the first Monday of December, unless by law they shall appoint a different day. This date was changed to January 3, by the Twentieth Amendment, dated January 23, 1933.

Article I, Section 5: Establishes the policy for each house to set up its own rules for judging elections, returns, and qualifications of its own members. Each house shall keep a journal.

This section spells out the rules for keeping records in both houses. It also spells out that neither house, during the session of Congress, shall, without consent of the other, adjourn for more than three days nor to any place other than where the two houses shall be sitting.

Article I, Section 6: Covers the compensation of representatives and senators.

Compensation shall be determined by law.

The Twenty-Seventh Amendment, which first was proposed in the late eighteenth century but not ratified until May 7, 1992, states that no law changing the compensation of senators and representatives shall take effect until the beginning of the next set of terms of office for representatives.

Article I, Section 7: All bills for raising revenue shall originate in the House of Representatives, but the Senate may propose or concur with amendments as on other bills. Every bill having passed both the House and Senate shall be presented to the president for approval.

The House has the lead on bills for raising revenue such as taxes, and the Senate may propose or concur with amendments, as with other bills. When the bill has passed both the House and Senate, the bill goes to the president for action.

Article I, Section 8: *These are the enumerated powers of the Federal Government, and no other powers are granted to Congress but are retained by the states and the people. This is spelled out clearly in the Tenth Amendment. This is a very impor-tant part of the Constitution, but over time it has become unclear exactly what these powers are. Perhaps these powers should be clarified during future conventions so that we all know exactly what they mean and allow. It may take a long time to finally arrive at an acceptable solution to the wording.*

1. Congress shall have the power to lay and collect taxes, duties, imposts and excises; to pay debts and provide for the common defense and general welfare of the United States, all uniform within the United States, and further to:
2. borrow money on the credit of the United States
3. regulate commerce with foreign nations, among the several states and with Indian tribes

Enumerated power Number 3 is the Commerce Clause, which has been used for justifying certain bills. It's really about the flow of products and services among the states, foreign countries, and Indian tribes. It has nothing to do with which products or services citizens should or should not be required to purchase. Such an interpretation is an infringement on liberty and freedom and should be rejected.

4. establish a uniform Rule of Naturalization
5. establish uniform laws on the subject of bankruptcies throughout the United States
6. coin money, regulate the value thereof, and of foreign coin, and fix the standard of weights and measures
7. provide for the punishment of counterfeiting the securities and current coin of the United States
8. establish post offices and post roads
9. promote the progress of science and useful arts, and protect exclusive rights to respective writings and discoveries
10. constitute tribunals inferior to the Supreme Court
11. define and punish piracies and felonies committed on the high seas and offenses against the law of nations
12. declare war, grant letters of marque and reprisal, and make rules concerning captures on land and water

*Congress has the power to declare war. No one else has this
power, not even the president.*

13. raise and support armies, but no appropriation shall be
for longer than two years

We need to add the Air Force now that we have one!

14. provide and maintain a navy

15. make rules for the government and regulation of the land
and naval forces

*This may be the place to authorize certain federal military
agencies such as the Army, Navy, Air Force, and the Department
of Defense, along with the associated secretaries.*

16. provide for the calling forth of the militia and to execute
the laws of the union, suppress insurrections, and repel
invasions

17. provide for organizing, arming, and disciplining the
militia, and for governing such part of them as may be
employed in the service of the United States, and reserving to the states the authority to appoint officers, and for
training the militia according to the discipline prescribed
by Congress

18. exercise exclusive legislation over the District of Columbia and exercise like authority of all places purchased by
the consent of the state in which the same shall be for
the erection of forts, magazines, arsenals, dockyards, and
other needful buildings

19. make all laws that shall be necessary and proper for
carrying into execution the foregoing powers and all

other powers vested by this Constitution in the government of the United States, or in any department or officer thereof

The Constitution is not clear on which other powers have been vested in the government of the United States or department or officer thereof; and consequently this is a subject for further debate and perhaps an amendment to clarify these other powers.

Article I, Section 9: The migration or importation of such persons as any of the states now existing shall think proper to admit shall not be prohibited by the Congress prior to the year 1808.

Since we're well past the year 1808, we don't need to spend much time on this clause.

Article I, Section 10: No state shall enter into any treaty, alliance, or confederation; grant letters of marque or reprisal; coin money; emit bills of credit; make anything but gold or silver a tender in payment of debts; pass any bill of attainder, ex post facto law, or law impairing the obligation of contracts; or grant any title of nobility.

If anything, these are tasks for the Federal Government, not the states.

Article II, Section 1: The executive power shall be vested in a President of the United States of America. He shall hold his office for a term of four years, and, together with the vice president, chosen for a four-year term, be elected as follows.

The Constitution details the process by which electors vote for the offices of president and vice president and how the president of the Senate makes the outcome official.

Article II, Section 2: The president shall be commander in chief of the Army and Navy of the United States and of the militia of the several states, when called into the actual service of the United States.

The president should be the commander in chief of all military forces of the United States. Additional powers such as making treaties and appointments, and related functions are defined in the Constitution.

Article II, Section 3: The president shall from time to time give to the Congress information of the state of the union, and recommend for their consideration such measures as he shall judge necessary and expedient.

Additional relationships between the president and Congress are described in further detail in the Constitution.

Article II, Section 4: The president, vice president, and all civil officers of the United States shall be removed from office on impeachment for, and conviction of, treason, bribery, or other high crimes and misdemeanors.

Article III, Section 1: The judicial power of the United States shall be vested in one Supreme Court and in such inferior courts as the Congress may from time to time ordain and establish.

The judges, both of the Supreme Court and inferior courts, shall hold their offices during good behavior, and shall, at stated times, receive for their services a compensation that shall not be diminished during their continuance in office.

Article III, Section 2: Judicial power shall extend to all cases, in law and equity, arising under this Constitution, the laws of the United States, and treaties made, or which shall be made, under their authority:

to all cases affecting ambassadors, other public ministers, and consuls; to all cases of admiralty and maritime jurisdiction; to controversies to which the United States shall be a party; to controversies between two or more states; between a state and a citizens of another state; between citizens of different states; between citizens of the same state claiming lands under grants of different states; and between a state, or a citizen thereof, and foreign states, citizens, or subjects.

In all cases affecting ambassadors, other public ministers and consuls, and those in which a state shall be party, the Supreme Court shall have original jurisdiction. In all other cases before mentioned, the Supreme Court shall have appellate jurisdiction, both as to law and fact, with such exceptions and under such regulations as Congress shall make.

The trial of all crimes, except in cases of impeachment, shall be by jury, and such a trial shall be held in the state where the said crimes were committed. When the crime was not committed with any state, the trial shall be at such place or places as Congress may by law have directed.

Article III, Section 3: Treason against the United States shall consist only in levying war against them or in adhering to their enemies or by giving them aid and comfort.

No person shall be convicted of treason unless upon the testimony of two witnesses to the same overt act or upon confession in open court.

Congress shall have the power to declare the punishment of treason, but no attainder of treason shall work corruption of blood or forfeiture except during the life of the person attained. "Corruption of blood" occurs when a person is convicted of treason and the Federal Government punishes the person's innocent family members. This is against the law and is described in Article 3, Section 3, Clause 2 of the US Constitution.

Article IV, Section 1: Full faith and credit shall be given in each state to the public acts, records, and judicial proceedings of every other state. The Congress may by general laws prescribe the manner in which such acts, records, and proceedings shall be proved, and the effect thereof.

Article IV, Section 2: The citizens of each state shall be entitled to all privileges and immunities of citizens of the states.

A person charged in any state with treason, felony, or other crime who flees from justice and is found in another state shall, on demand of the executive authority of the state from which he fled, be delivered up to be removed to the state that has jurisdiction of the crime.

Furthermore, no person held to service or labor in one state, under the laws thereof, who escapes into another, shall, in consequence of any law or regulation therein, be discharged from such service or labor, but shall be delivered up on claim of the party to whom such service or labor may be due.

Article IV, Section 3: New states may be admitted by Congress into the union, but no new state shall be formed or erected within the jurisdiction of any other state; nor shall any state be formed by the junction of two or more states, or parts of states, without the consent of the legislatures of the states concerned as well as of Congress.

Congress shall have the power to dispose of and make all needful rules and regulations respecting the territory or other property belonging to the United States, and nothing in the Constitution shall be so construed as to prejudice any claims of the United States or of any particular state.

Article IV, Section 4: The United States shall guarantee to every state in this union a republican form of government and shall protect each of them against invasion, and on application of the legislature, or of the executive (when the legislature cannot be convened) against domestic violence.

Article V: The Congress, whenever two-thirds of both houses shall deem it necessary, shall propose amendments to this Constitution, or, on the application of the legislatures of two-thirds of the several states, shall call a convention for proposing amendments, which, in either case, shall be valid to all intents and purposes as part of this Constitution, when ratified by the legislatures of three-fourths of the several states, or by the conventions in three-fourths thereof, as the one or other mode of ratification may be proposed by the Congress.

(This is provided that no amendment made prior to the year 1808 shall in any manner affect the first and fourth clauses in the ninth section of the first article and that no state, without its consent, shall be deprived of its equal suffrage in the Senate.)

Article VI: All debts contracted and engagements entered into before the adoption of this Constitution shall be valid against the United States under this Constitution, as under the confederation.

The Constitution and the laws of the United States, which shall be made in pursuance thereof—and all treaties made, or which shall be made, under the authority of the United States—shall be the supreme law of the land. The judges in every state shall be bound by anything in the Constitution or the laws of any state to the contrary notwithstanding.

The senators and representatives before mentioned, and the members of the several state legislatures, and all executive and judicial officers, both of the United States and of the states, shall be bound by oath or affirmation to support the Constitution, but no religious test shall ever be required as a qualification to any office or public trust under the United States.

Article VII: The ratification of the convention of nine states shall be sufficient for the establishment of this Constitution between the states so ratifying the same.

Done in Convention by the Unanimous Consent of the States present the Seventeenth Day of September in the Year of our Lord one thousand seven hundred and Eighty seven and of the Independence of the United States of America the Twelfth In witness whereof We have hereunto subscribed our Names,

G. WASHINGTON, president and deputy from Virginia

[The Constitution also was signed by the deputies of twelve states. Rhode Island did not sign, as it had not yet ratified the Constitution; it did so on May 29, 1790.]

AMENDING THE CONSTITUTION

The founders knew that the Constitution contained flaws and would need to be amended to correct those flaws. Specifically they knew that the first ten amendments, also known as the Bill of Rights, needed to be incorporated into the Constitution very soon. They also realized that issues would arise in the future and would need to be addressed for compliance with the Constitution or for amending the Constitution.

For these reasons they incorporated Article V into the Constitution in order to be able to make, at any future time, changes that would correct flaws and create a more perfect document. The founders also knew they could not possibly be aware of future advances in all aspects of new knowledge and how these changes might affect the Constitution. Future leaders would address such new issues. Above all the founders wanted to be sure that the country remained, as Abraham Lincoln later stated, a government "of the people, by the people, and for the people that shall not perish from the earth."

As stated in Article V, amending the Constitution is a two-step process of proposition and ratification. There are two ways to propose an amendment. One is by a two-thirds vote in favor of a proposed amendment in both houses of Congress, assuming the presence of a quorum in both houses. All ratified and un-ratified amendments have been proposed by this method. The second way is for Congress to call for a convention to propose amendments when requested by at least two thirds of the states, currently thirty-four. No amendments have ever been proposed by this method.

Following approval in Congress or in a convention to propose amendments, a proposed amendment must then be ratified. There are two possible methods of ratification; only Congress may choose which method to use. One method is ratification by the legislatures of three-fourths of the states. Such proposals sometimes, but not always, have a ratification deadline. The other method is by a convention of three-fourths of the states. Only the Twenty-First Amendment, which repealed the Eighteenth Amendment prohibiting alcohol, was ratified in this manner.

To summarize, all of the proposals to amend the Constitution from 1787 to date have been initiated by the Congress, none by a states' convention for proposing amendments. All except one of the ratified proposals have been ratified by three-fourths of state legislatures and only one has been ratified by a states' convention.

It is also important to know that the President of the United States has no role in the Constitutional amendment process. He is on the sidelines and may have indirect influence over amendment proposals through favorable or unfavorable personal comments in private or in public, but he has no direct influence.

The President is the chief executive officer with a responsibility to defend the Constitution, but he has no say in amending the Constitution itself. Changes to the Constitution occur through the approval of the Congress and the states, and the people through the states.

Article V also specifies certain clauses that cannot be amended by the usual process. The first two restrictions, regarding slave trade and taxes, expired in 1808 and are no longer applicable. The last one specifies that an amendment cannot deprive a state of equal representation in the Senate without the state's approval; this restriction still applies today.

THE RATIFIED AMENDMENTS

Let's take a look at how we as a nation have changed our Constitution in terms of the twenty-seven amendments ratified since the final ratification of the Constitution by Rhode Island on May 29, 1790. Of the twenty-seven amendments, one amendment, the Twenty-First, repealed another, the Eighteenth, so we have a net number of twenty-five amendments to date that cover nearly a quarter of a millennium.

Below are brief descriptions of the twenty-seven amendments that have been ratified as of this writing in 2012. The date following each amendment is the date of ratification. The full text of the twenty-seven amendments appears in Appendix IV.

First Amendment: protects the freedoms of religion, speech, and the press, as well as the right to assemble and petition the government. December 15, 1791.

Second Amendment: protects an individual's right to bear arms. December 15, 1791.

Third Amendment: prohibits the forced quartering of soldiers outside of wartime. December 15, 1791.

Fourth Amendment: prohibits unreasonable searches and seizures and sets out requirements for search warrants based on probable cause. December 15, 1791.

Fifth Amendment: sets out rules for indictment by grand jury and eminent domain, protects the right to due process, and prohibits self-incrimination and double jeopardy. December 15, 1791.

Sixth Amendment: protects the right to a fair and speedy public trial by jury, including the rights to be notified of the accusations, to confront the accuser, to obtain witnesses, and to retain counsel. December 15, 1791.

Seventh Amendment: provides for the right to a trial by jury in certain civil cases, according to common law. December 15, 1791.

Eighth Amendment: prohibits excessive fines and excessive bail as well as cruel and unusual punishment. December 15, 1791.

Ninth Amendment: protects rights not enumerated in the Constitution. December 15, 1791.

Tenth Amendment: limits the powers of the Federal Government to those delegated to it by the Constitution. December 15, 1791.

The first ten amendments are called the Bill of Rights.

Eleventh Amendment: provides immunity to states from lawsuits from out-of-state citizens and foreigners not living within the states' borders; lays the foundation for sovereign immunity. February 7, 1795.

Twelfth Amendment: revises presidential election procedures. June 15, 1804.

Thirteenth Amendment: abolishes slavery and involuntary servitude, except as punishment for a crime. December 6, 1865.

Fourteenth Amendment: defines citizenship; contains the privileges or immunities clause, the due process clause, and the equal protection clause; and deals with post–Civil War issues. July 9, 1868.

Fifteenth Amendment: prohibits the denial of the right to vote based on race, color, or previous condition of servitude. February 3, 1870.

Sixteenth Amendment: allows the Federal Government to collect taxes on income. February 3, 1913.

Seventeenth Amendment: establishes the direct election of US senators by popular vote. April 8, 1913.

Eighteenth Amendment: establishes the prohibition of alcohol. (This was repealed by the Twenty-First Amendment.) January 16, 1919.

Nineteenth Amendment: establishes women's suffrage. August 18, 1920.

Twentieth Amendment: fixes the dates of term commencements for members of Congress (January 3) and the president (January 20). This amendment is also known as the "lame duck amendment." January 23, 1933.

Twenty-First Amendment: repeals the Eighteenth Amendment. December 5, 1933.

Twenty-Second Amendment: limits presidential terms to two, or a maximum of ten years (i.e., if a vice president serves not more than one-half of a president's term, he or she can be elected to two more terms). February 27, 1951.

Twenty-Third Amendment: provides for representation of Washington, DC, in the Electoral College. March 29, 1961.

Twenty-Fourth Amendment: prohibits the revocation of voting rights due to the nonpayment of poll taxes. January 23, 1964.

Twenty-Fifth Amendment: codifies the Tyler Precedent and defines the process of presidential succession. February 10, 1967.

John Tyler, the first vice president to replace a sitting president, established a pattern that was followed for well over a century. Until the "Tyler Precedent," it was unclear precisely how the nation would replace a president who died in office. John Tyler was the first vice president to show how important the person in the job could become.

Twenty-Sixth Amendment: sets the official voting age at eighteen years old. July 1, 1971.

Twenty-Seventh Amendment: prevents laws affecting Congressional salary from taking effect until the beginning of the next session of Congress. May 5 or 7, 1992.

A REVIEW OF
NON-RATIFIED PROPOSALS

The following paragraphs are an overview of proposals that were not ratified, those that are awaiting ratification, and those that were not approved by Congress in the nineteenth, twentieth, and twenty-first centuries.

There have been two proposals approved by Congress that have not been ratified. The first is the Equal Rights Amendment, approved by Congress in 1972, which would make government discrimination based on a person's sex illegal. At the end of the second deadline, June 30, 1982, a total of thirty-five of the required thirty-eight states had ratified the amendment, which was not sufficient for ratification. Some believe the deadline can be further extended, but so far it has not been. In recent years the proposal has come up again for extension, and two states appear to be ready to ratify it, but the action is still pending.

The second non-ratified proposal is the District of Columbia Voting Rights Amendment, approved on August 22, 1975, which would give the residents of the District of Columbia full representation in both houses of Congress in addition to full participation in the Electoral College. It expired in 1985 with only sixteen states ratifying it before the deadline. No further action on this proposal has been planned.

There are four amendments approved by Congress that are still open for ratification. All of these proposed amendments are still technically active and never have expired; thus the state legislatures could ratify them at any time. The first is the Congressional Apportionment Amendment, which Congress approved in 1789 as part of the proposed Bill of Rights. This is the only one of twelve amendments proposed in the original Bill of Rights that never has been ratified by the states. It specifies how the seats in the House should be apportioned and so far has been ratified by eleven states; one state, Delaware, rejected it in 1790.

In 1810, Congress approved the Title of Nobility Amendment. This amendment would revoke the citizenship of anyone who accepted a foreign title of nobility. Twelve states ratified it; three rejected it.

The Corwin Amendment was approved by Congress in 1861. This amendment sought to protect slavery from federal intervention and was an effort to avert the outbreak of the Civil War. Thomas Corwin was the twentieth United States Secretary of the Treasury. Practically no action has been taken on this issue since the outbreak of the Civil War on April 12, 1861.

Finally, the Child Labor Amendment, approved by Congress in 1924, would give Congress exclusive authority to enact child labor laws. This was essentially a power play that would give Congress power over the states in child labor matters.

Twenty-eight states ratified it while twelve rejected it, making ratification virtually improbable.

Next we will take a look at some of the many proposed amendments Congress did not approve. There have been more than 11,000 such proposals to amend the Constitution from 1789 to the present. All of these proposals were introduced by a member of Congress but either died in a committee or did not received the required two-thirds vote in both houses of Congress to go to the states for ratification.

During the nineteenth century, more than 1,800 proposals were submitted before Congress but did not go forward. Three noteworthy proposals were the Crittenden Compromise, the Christian Amendment, and the Blaine Amendment. The Crittenden Compromise was a joint resolution that included six constitutional amendments that would have protected slavery. Both houses rejected the proposal in 1861, and Abraham Lincoln was elected on a platform that opposed the expansion of slavery. The South's reaction to the amendment's rejection paved the way for the secession of the Confederate states and the start of the US Civil War.

The Christian Amendment was first proposed in February 1863 and would have added the acknowledgment of the Christian God to the preamble to the Constitution. Similar proposals were made in 1874, 1896, and 1910, but none passed. The last attempt was in 1954 and did not come to a vote.

The Blaine Amendment was proposed in 1875 and would have banned public funds from going to religious purposes. This was a move by some to prevent Catholics from taking advantage of such funds. Although it failed to pass in Congress, many states have adopted such provisions to their own constitutions.

In the twentieth century, a large number of proposals were submitted to Congress for approval but did not go forward. Some of the more notable ones include the following. The Anti-Miscegenation Amendment, proposed by Seaborn Rodden-berry in 1912, forbids interracial marriages across the country. Similar amendments were proposed by Congressman Andrew King in 1871 and Senator Coleman Blease in 1928. None of these were passed by Congress.

Proposed in 1951 by Ohio Senator John W. Bricker, the Bricker Amendment would have limited the federal government's treaty-making power. It received sixty yea votes and thirty-one nays, one vote short of the two-thirds required.

Texas Representative Henry Gonzalez proposed the Death Penalty Abolition Amendment in 1990, 1992, 1993, and 1995. Its purpose was to prohibit the imposition of capital punishment by any state, territory, or other jurisdiction within the United States. Each time, the proposal was referred to the House Subcommittee on the Constitution but never made it out of committee.

Another proposal in the twentieth century was the Flag Desecration Amendment, which was proposed several times and passed the House several times but never the Senate. This is a controversial proposal that would allow Congress to statutorily prohibit expression of political views through the physical desecration of the flag of the United States. While this proposal is often referred to as "flag burning," the language would permit the prohibition of all forms of flag desecration, which may take forms other than burning, such as using the flag for clothing or napkins. In 2006, however, the Senate voted sixty-six in support and thirty-four opposed, one vote short of the two-thirds necessary for passage.

Finally, the Human Life Amendment, first introduced in 1973, aimed to overturn the *Roe v. Wade* Supreme Court ruling regarding abortion. Since then it was introduced more than three hundred times with various wording; in all but one case it died in committee. The one time that it went to a floor vote as the Hatch Eagleton Amendment, the Senate rejected it by eighteen votes.

In the twenty-first century, members of Congress have submitted a number of notable proposals, but like those described above, these proposals never made it out of committee or with two-thirds approval of both houses. Some of the more notable proposals include the Balanced Budget Amendment, which has been introduced many times but has never gone forward; the School Prayer Amendment, which would give the people the right to pray and to recognize their religious beliefs, heritage, and traditions on public property, and schools; and the Every Vote Counts Amendment, which would abolish the Electoral College and allow the popular vote to determine the outcome of presidential elections.

Also, the Federal Marriage Amendment was introduced several times. It would define marriage and prohibit same-sex marriage even at the state level. In addition an amendment that would repeal the Twenty-Second Amendment was introduced by representatives and a senator; it would repeal the two-term limit for a president. The last action was in 2009, but it has not gone forward. In 2009 Senator Jim DeMint proposed term limits for the United States Congress. The amendment would limit senators to two terms (twelve years) and representatives to three terms (six years).

None of the above noteworthy proposals have gone forward to the states for ratification; they either have been shelved or died due to a time limit. Furthermore all 11,000 or so proposals submitted for amending the Constitution since 1789 have been submitted by members of Congress, none by the people through the states. We need to take a hard look at what this means for our country.

WHERE DO WE STAND TODAY?

Let's analyze the amendments. The first ten amendments, called the Bill of Rights, were well defined even prior to the final ratification of the Constitution. In fact they were the reason Rhode Island delayed so long in ratifying the Constitution. Rhode Island wanted to make sure these amendments would be incorporated into the Constitution before the state ratified it.

Note that the Twenty-Seventh Amendment was proposed on September 25, 1789 but not approved until May 7, 1992 and that it's the last amendment to be ratified and approved. Two amendments cancel each other out, the Eighteenth and the Twenty-First. This leaves only fourteen amendments proposed and ratified after the Constitution was originally ratified in 1790.

Three amendments deal with the issue of suffrage. The Fifteenth Amendment prohibits the denial of suffrage based on race, color, or prior servitude. The Nineteenth provides for women's suffrage, and the Twenty-Sixth sets the voting age at eighteen years old. These were not issues during the debates by the founders. This leaves eleven amendments that were not original issues for the founders.

Amendments Thirteen, Fourteen, and Fifteen cover issues that arose from the Civil War. The Thirteenth abolishes slavery; the Fourteenth defines citizenship and overrules the 1857 *Dred Scott v. Sandford* ruling by the Supreme Court; and the Fifteenth provides the right to vote regardless of race, color, or previous condition of servitude. Again, these amendments are all related to the Civil War. Take these three away, and we have eight left to analyze.

The remaining eight amendments are not earth shattering. The Sixteenth Amendment allows Congress to collect income tax. The Seventeenth changes the selection of senators from state legislations to a majority vote by the people. The Twentieth fixes the beginning and ending of the terms of elected federal offices. The Twenty-Second limits the president to two terms in office. The Twenty-Third gives Washington, DC, votes in the Electoral College. The Twenty-Fourth prohibits requiring a poll tax to vote. The Twenty-Fifth defines presidential succession, and the Twenty-Seventh moves the beginning of congressional salary changes to the start of the next session of Congress.

You may think that all of the amendments that follow the first ten are simple and straightforward and should have no cause for alarm or controversy; in fact, some of them may be a cause for concern. The Seventeenth Amendment, which changes the way senators are elected, was inconsistent with states rights; it also eliminated important advantages of state influence over the Senate. Senators should be elected by state legislatures so that the Federal Government will be more beholden to states' rights. With popular voting, senators are more inclined to be beholden to their political parties, and this allows the parties to have too much power. In addition, the Twenty-Sixth amendment, which sets the voting age at eighteen years, is also not well served. Eighteen is much too young to vote, and many people believe the voting age should be increased to at least twenty-one. Just because an eighteen-year-old man can be drafted for war does not mean he is wise enough to vote, and therefore he should not be asked to take on this responsibility until he is more experienced with the world.

Other than the foregoing statements on the impact of the twenty-seven amendments, our amendment process has not made any positive changes to correct ambiguities or other issues that we have had as a nation since the Constitution originally was ratified. It should be clear to all Americans that a constitution should be clear and unequivocal and should not be subject to interpretation for an advantage by one faction over another. This is what we are dealing with today.

WHAT YOU CAN DO FOR YOUR COUNTRY

We must ask ourselves exactly what we want our Constitution to do for us. The founders laid out their goals to establish justice, ensure domestic tranquility, promote the general welfare, and secure the blessings of liberty to ourselves and our posterity. In simpler terms, they wanted freedom and justice for all, forever.

The opposite of this meant living under a monarchy, which is what the early settlers left in Europe and England but were finding out that they hadn't escaped sufficiently. By the late 1700s, the King of England was still in charge, and the people were without freedom. The king made the rules, and the people had to follow them. So our founders declared independence, and we fought and won a war so we could have our freedom.

The founders worked very long and hard to finally arrive at the finished draft of the Constitution. When the draft was completed, they weren't satisfied that they had everything right. In order to make a start without further delay, however, they incorporated Article V into the Constitution to provide the basis for amendments that they expected would be added in the future to make our country a more perfect union.

Our target is freedom and freedom for those who follow. We also need to qualify that our freedom comes with responsibility. This means we must be fair and honest in our dealings with one another. All people are born equal in the eyes of our creator, but not everyone is equal in terms of ability. Some are more motivated than others; some are more intelligent than others; some are more carefree than others; some are a different race than others; some are more articulate than others; and some are physically stronger than others. In other words, we are not all equal in all ways, but we are all different from one another. With everyone different, we have a vibrant society and an interesting and exciting country. If everyone were the same, how dull it would be. We should be thankful for the differences among us. Moreover, if we're willing, we can all get along together in our different ways under the banner of a free society.

Under a monarchy, the situation is quite different. A king or dictator is in charge of everyone. He has the power of life and death over his subjects. He has the power to choose who will be his friends and who will be his serfs. His friends have great power and property, given by the monarch for loyalty. There is no way to achieve power except through the monarch. There is no freedom and no way to find it. The original British settlers came here for freedom, and we want to keep it that way for ourselves and our posterity. However, freedom is not free but must be fought for constantly. This is where we find ourselves today, and we must be aware of changing times and take appropriate action.

What is a monarchy? Is it one man, one woman, a dictator, a tyrant, a president, or something else? Could it be a central government that has become too powerful and is taking control of the lives of its people? Could the government be an authority that has the power of life or death over its subjects? This was a central theme debated over and over during the time of the founding fathers. Some wanted a powerful Federal Government while others wanted a much less powerful Federal Government. Those who wanted a less powerful Federal Government were afraid it might become more like a monarchy and would take away the people's freedom.

Some would argue that our government has moved toward a stronger Federal Government over the past many years and is now approaching unprecedented power over the people. In fact it has been moving in that direction so quietly that we barely notice it is happening. Could the US Federal Government now be approaching the power of a monarchy?

If this is so, have we come all this way only to return to the same condition that our ancestors endured when they decided to come to this land in the first place? Why did the founders declare independence from England, and why did we fight the Revolutionary War? Why did the founders write a constitution that would set us free for ourselves and our posterity? Why did they spend so much time debating the pros and cons as to how much power the Federal Government should have? Why were some founders afraid to give the Federal Government too much power, and why were the powers given finally enumerated in Article I, Section 8, of the Constitution? Finally, why did the founders incorporate Article V into the Constitution?

Most of the answers to these questions are obvious in that these actions were taken to guarantee our freedoms and the freedoms of our posterity. Article V was incorporated to provide a process to make amendments to the Constitution that come to light in view of new conditions in the world. When new conditions come into conflict with the Constitution, we find it necessary to amend the Constitution in order to guarantee freedom and ensure that we have a more perfect union. After all, the Constitution is the primary law of the land. We need to be able to make changes to the Constitution to reflect changes in the world as time passes. This means changes in technology, language, culture, and other influences that impact the lives of all citizens. The fact that we have ratified only twenty-seven amendments over the past 235 years or so tells us we have a very cumbersome amendment process and have been stymied in our attempts to make meaningful and positive changes that would benefit the country. More important, most of the amendments have had little effect on the overall course of the country. In other words, they have had little impact on guaranteeing our freedoms and the freedoms of our posterity. We need to correct this now.

Let's take a look at Article V of the Constitution_in its entirety and analyze the text of this article.

Article V

The Congress, whenever two thirds of both Houses shall deem it necessary, shall propose Amendments to this Constitution, or, on the Application of the Legislatures of two thirds of the several States, shall call a Convention for proposing Amendments, which, in either Case, shall be valid to all Intents and Purposes, as Part of this Constitution, when ratified by the Legislators of three fourths of the several States, or by Conventions in three fourths thereof, as the one or the other Mode of Ratification may be proposed by the Congress; provided that no Amendment which may be made prior to the Year One thousand eight hundred and eight shall in any Manner affect the first and fourth Clauses in the Ninth Section of the first Article; and that no State, without its Consent, shall be deprived of its equal Suffrage in the Senate.

Article V is a bit difficult to digest, but let's try. A two-thirds approval of a proposed amendment in both the House and Senate—or an application by two-thirds of the legislatures of several states for Congress to call a convention for proposing amendments—qualifies for Congress to make a call. The call is to send the proposed amendments, either those approved by both houses of Congress, or those from a states' convention for proposals, to the States for ratification, or a call for a convention of at least two-thirds of the states to ratify the proposed amendments. The Constitution, however, does not specify who in Congress shall make the call for a convention to either propose or ratify, and this must be clarified.

The 11,000 or so measures that have been proposed to amend the Constitution from 1789 to the present—excluding the twenty-seven that have been ratified—were all introduced by a member of Congress and either died in committee or did not receive a two-thirds vote in both houses of Congress and were therefore not sent to the states for ratification. This suggests that it is easy for a member of Congress to submit a proposal to amend the Constitution but difficult to achieve a two-thirds approval in both houses on any matter. This isn't surprising!

To date, all of the activity regarding amending the Constitution has occurred within Congress, with no proposals coming from conventions called for making proposals to amend the Constitution. No amendments have ever been ratified that have been proposed from a convention for proposing amendments resulting from an application from two-thirds of the several states. Among other reasons for this, there is no clear chain of command in the Congress for taking action on any application by two-thirds of the states for Congress to call a convention for proposing amendments. Article V states that Congress shall take action on proposals, but it does not designate who in Congress is responsible for this. With no one responsible, and with 535 members of Congress, who is supposed to step up to the plate? It is plain to see why no proposed amendment ever has been submitted by a convention for proposing amendments and processed accordingly. This needs to be addressed and clarified by an amendment to Article V that designates a point of contact in Congress responsible for taking action on applications from the states for a convention to propose amendments by at least two-thirds of the states. This individual could be the Speaker of the House, for example.

This country needs a process for processing all proposals for amendments to the Constitution; we never have had a workable process, and consequently, many proposals are never acted upon. Since only proposals initiated within Congress have ever been ratified, and no proposals submitted through states' conventions have ever been ratified, we are simply not able to give anyone who is not a member of Congress a voice in amending the Constitution. We need to establish a process that will change this.

Our founders gave us the means and authority to do this under Article V, but we have been unsuccessful in making it happen. The process spelled out in Article V states that when two-thirds of state legislatures submit a request to Congress for a convention to propose amendments to the Constitution, Congress shall call a states' convention to do this. Since this has never occurred, here is the dilemma. If the people want to have a say in the direction this country will take, they should work through their state legislatures to make this process available to all citizens who are registered to vote, and they should publicize the process through all media.

If the only parties who actually make proposed amendments to the Constitution are the 535 members of Congress, we never will be able to make changes to the Constitution that are unfavorable to those members. These issues could be related to congressional pay, perks, term limits, or other issues that benefit only members of Congress. On the other hand, if proposed amendments do not benefit individual members of Congress in any way, they are less likely to make the effort to move forward with such proposals. This is a matter of power, in that Congress has the de facto power to maintain the status quo regarding amendment proposals, and they will retain that power until challenged by the people.

Our founders were smart and wise men who saw through this dilemma, and this is why they added the alternative process of taking applications from state legislatures for proposing amendments. With this in mind, where would our country be today if we had made more use of processing amendments initiated by the people through state conventions and these amendments subsequently had been ratified? The answer is a different Constitution than we have today, and a better one in terms of achieving more perfect union.

Each state must develop a process to encourage citizens to submit proposals for amending the Constitution and sorting out and analyzing each one. This will not be an easy task and will require a great deal of thought from many intelligent people. Undoubtedly, any process will be handled from private citizens through their state legislative representative to a central collection office at the state level, and from there recorded, evaluated, and filed for action when appropriate. In addition, states will have to work together more effectively to determine when they should contact Congress to call for a convention and to identify which proposals to offer to the convention. A convention once every ten years would be a good start; this could be an event with a periodic recurrence, much like the US Census. Moreover, the requirements for this convention could even be outlined in an amendment to the Constitution. All states likely would welcome this proposal and vote favorably.

For the states to make this happen, they would have to work more closely together. By working together, states would benefit by gaining more support from the public and more power to deal with the Federal Government. Federal power versus state power has been an issue since the founding of our country, and the Feds have had the upper hand by far. This is a conundrum that must be addressed and fixed. The states could have more power if they worked together and forced Congress to call a convention whenever the states had amendments to propose. Again this is spelled out clearly in Article V and is the alternate amendment proposal process. However, this has never occurred since the first convention that gave us the original Constitution in 1787.

Moreover, for a convention for proposing amendments to be effective and successful, it must have a rational protocol to establish the rules by which the convention will be conducted. This will take considerable study and expertise in conducting large-scale meetings, as the conventions likely will be made up of delegates from each state equal to the number of Congressional representatives. It will be most important to limit the convention to a workable number of proposals in order to be able to actually arrive at a definite conclusion for each proposal that will go forward for ratification. For example, a convention may be limited to one proposal or a fixed not-to-exceed number of proposals. This number, and its wording, must be crafted very carefully by the people in charge of the convention for the outcome to be successful and also must be clearly announced prior to the convention.

For any of this to occur, it will take the effort of all citizens to contact their state and federal representatives repeatedly to make it a high priority. We have not yet had citizens directly involved in the amendment process, but now is the time for it to happen. If we want to return to the founders' concept for our country, which is to have both a federal and state government structure, with limited federal powers, and all other powers remaining with the states and the people, we must act now. This action will put all citizens in contact with our country's governance, even if indirectly.

FUTURE AMENDMENTS TO THE CONSTITUTION

Deciding on future amendments to the Constitution is the difficult part, but there is no immediate hurry. After all, the Constitution has been working; it just needs to be updated and refined. What are the issues that need to be addressed and what are the priorities? Which parts of the Constitution need to be repealed, amended, or left alone? Let's take a look at the Constitution first; next, look at the twenty-seven amendments; then review proposals that already have been submitted but did not go forward; and finally examine recommendations for amendment proposals.

In general the Constitution that was ratified in 1787 has been a good standard for the country. Most of the wording is appropriate and well stated. Certain issues, however, must be addressed to clarify ambiguities and misunderstandings.

Article I, Section 6 states that senators and representatives shall receive a compensation for their services, to be ascertained by law. In this case, who makes the law? Congress makes the law, and as such, members of Congress decide on their own compensation. We need to see some reference to a requirement that compensation should be related to a specific formula. After all, Congress works for the taxpayers, so the taxpayers should have a say in the compensation formula. A formula for this purpose could be incorporated into the Constitution.

In Article I, Section 8, the clause "to regulate Commerce with foreign Nations, and among the several States, and with the Indian Tribes" is known as the Commerce Clause and has many interpretations. This clause should apply to the flow of commerce across state and foreign boundaries and not the authority to determine who must purchase certain products or services. This clause needs clarification to avoid unconstitutional legislation.

Furthermore, any clauses related to the declaration of war, the making of rules for government, and the regulation of the military forces should include the addition of the United States Air Force and the Department of Defense, all added to our armed forces since the ratification of the original Constitution. Moreover, the militia is referenced numerous times but is not the appropriate term today; therefore all such military references should be changed to the more current terms "National Guard" and "reserve forces," as applicable.

Article II, Section 1, which states that the president shall be the commander in chief of the Army and Navy and of the militia of the states when called into service of the United States, should be modified to incorporate the current breakdown of the military services (i.e., it should include the Department of Defense, the US Air Force, and the National Guard).

Finally, Article V needs clarification in terms of who in Congress shall call for conventions requested by the states for making proposals to amend the Constitution. Since no one has this responsibility, no convention has ever been called for this purpose, and consequently no proposals for amending the Constitution ever have been made by the states. This clause needs to be changed, and someone in Congress should be designated with the authority to call conventions when two-thirds of the states request a convention. Without someone in Congress responsible for this duty, requests are simply ignored, and Congress has been able to retain the power to make all amendments to the Constitution. This is truly a matter of power that so far has been in the hands of Congress and not the people. To correct this, whenever two-thirds of the states request a convention for amending the Constitution, a call for the convention must be automatic with no questions asked.

More urgent, however, is a need for an amendment to Article V that calls for a Convention for proposing amendments to take place every ten years, similar to census-taking, so that a convention of states to propose amendments would be automatic. This proposal would no doubt be ratified by most, if not all, of the states and give the states a stronger role in governing the country, as visualized by the founders. It could propose to begin the first such convention within one year following ratification of the proposed amendment by three-fourths of the states. By doing this, the individual states always would have sufficient time to plan for the next convention and be prepared for a successful outcome.

There are, no doubt, many other issues that need to be addressed, but the foregoing are priorities. Once we have a more workable system for processing amendments, the country probably will have more and better proposals for amendments that make sense and have a positive impact.

Now that we have reviewed the original Constitution, let's focus on the amendments that already have been ratified over the past two hundred or so years. Some of the amendments are candidates for further review and possible change. These are discussed in the following paragraphs.

The first ten amendments are the Bill of Rights. None of these are candidates for change or amendment.

The Seventeenth Amendment changed the selection of senators from state legislatures to the popular vote. The founders wanted the states to select senators in order to give the states more influence by having a direct link with their senators. With our current popular-vote election of senators, the states have lost their influence, and political parties have become more powerful. The founders were very conscious of the dichotomy, or contrast, of federal power versus state power. They did not want federal power to trump the power of the states, so they enumerated specific federal powers in Article I, Section 8; all other powers returned to the states or the people. For this reason the founders wanted the state legislatures to select their own senators. The Seventeenth Amendment reversed this and should be repealed so that state legislatures will again select their senators.

The Twenty-Sixth Amendment sets the voting age at eighteen years old. As mentioned, this is truly a mistake, as eighteen is simply too young to have the experience to know the issues and make a rational vote. This amendment was ratified to pacify young men and women who fought in wars at age eighteen; for that reason, these individuals argued that they should be eligible to vote. It is also suggested that the Twenty-Sixth Amendment was ratified to provide an advantage to candidates for office who would benefit from an electorate with less overall knowledge of current issues. We should seriously consider reversing this amendment and increase the voting age to twenty-one or even twenty-five, the age required to qualify as a US representative. We should not burden eighteen-year-olds with this responsibility. A few eighteen-year-olds would be mature enough but certainly not most.

The foregoing are two suggestions for consideration from those amendments that already have been ratified. Below are two further suggestions from among those proposals that have been submitted in the past but have not gone forward for ratification.

A Balanced Budget Amendment is certainly a candidate for ratification and ultimate approval by three-fourths of the states. This amendment would not allow the Federal Government to spend more than it takes in from revenues and ultimately would reduce the nation's debt to zero. In the meantime it would reduce the interest on the current debt we have on the books. This proposal has been submitted by members of Congress many times but has never gone forward through the Congress. It could be that Congress does not want to give up the power it has over debt and finance. This is the time for the states to get involved in this issue by submitting an amendment approved by two-thirds of the states to go forward to the ratification procedure.

Finally, the Federal Marriage Amendment is another candidate for amending the Constitution that needs to be in place. This is an issue that cannot be left up to the individual states but must apply to all of the states. If one state has a law that is not recognized in all other states, the country will have a major problem dealing with the differences. Once and for all, we should have a law that will cover all marriage issues and have it apply to all of the states on the same basis.

SUMMARY

This study has covered the history of world in a very brief over-view to give the reader perspective regarding where we are today in terms of government. We have discovered that the US Constitution has given more freedom to its citizens than any other form of government in history. In other words, we have achieved the ultimate in a government that provides freedom and equality to all of its citizens, and we have a constitution that is a living document that will protect our freedoms, if we are able to keep it that way.

On the other hand, human nature plays a pivotal role in how we manage power between the Federal Government and state governments. Our founders were bent on limiting the power of the Federal Government because they realized too much power there would lead to actions that are closely tied to a monarchy (e.g., wars, high taxes, more regulations, and less freedom). Over the years, however, our country has moved so slowly in this direction that we barely notice the changes taking place. The Federal Government has taken control of the country, and the states have lost their power. As a result we the people are less free than at any other time in the history of the United States of America.

Political power has moved away from the states to the Federal Government and the political parties. The political parties are under the influence of major contributors such as Wall Street, unions, large corporations, and other entities that fund the political parties and the 535 individual members of Congress for favors in return. Members of Congress, like any other group of people, follow the bell-shaped curve. Some are really good, some are fair to average, and some are just plain bad. The contributors to the political parties, along with the good, fair, and bad politicians, control the political power in this country, and as a consequence, the direction of the country. This direction is perhaps good for the few and bad for the many and this is what we need to address.

We can see this trend in the way Constitutional amendment proposals are processed. Instead of the states being involved in proposing amendments as specified in Article V of the Constitution, we know that the only avenue for this process has been through Congress alone. It doesn't take a rocket scientist to see that the Constitutional amendments that have so far been ratified somehow benefit Congress in one way or another. Those proposals that do not go forward for ratification are those that have no benefit for Congress. In other words, Congress decides the direction of the country, and the states or people do not. This is not the way the founders envisioned how the country would be governed, as we read from those who were there at the time of this nation's founding. Since our government exists to serve the people, the people should have a say in the governance of the country. One way for this to happen is for the people to have a say in the Constitutional amendments through their state legislatures, and Article V of the Constitution provides for this. Unfortunately this has never occurred, and Congress has retained de facto power over amending the Constitution.

Let's review the ratified amendments again. Discount the first ten, as they already were proposed and ready for ratification before the Constitution was ratified. Of the remaining seventeen, the Twenty-First cancels the Eighteenth on the subject of prohibition. The Thirteenth, Fourteenth, and Fifteenth relate to the outcome of the Civil War. The Twelfth, Twentieth, Twenty-Second, Twenty-Third, and Twenty-Fifth relate to presidential and Congressional term issues. The Eleventh is a judicial issue. None of these had any benefit to Congress but were issues that were important to the country and were very popular. All the rest (the Sixteenth, Seventeenth, Nineteenth, Twenty-Fourth, Twenty-Sixth, and Twenty-Seventh) were of definite benefit to Congress in terms of increasing the number of voters, making pay increases more favorable, and tax issues that relate to Congressional power.

There are no amendments that reduce the power or the perks of Congress. Moreover, as long as members of Congress submit all proposals for amendments, there will never be an amendment that reduces the perks or power of members of Congress. This is not what the founders envisioned for the country as per Article V, which provides for the two methods for proposals for amendments, one method resulting from a two-thirds vote in both houses of Congress, and the other from a request by two-thirds of the state legislatures for a convention to propose amendments. Since we have never had a convention for the states to propose amendments, we have a major problem that must be addressed.

NOW IT'S UP TO YOU

This is truly the time for everyone to get involved in our government. The Constitutional amendment process is one of the ways
by which all citizens can have an impact and be involved. You
can get involved by repeatedly contacting your state legislators to let them know you want action taken regarding having a
states' convention to propose amendments to the Constitution.
Let them know that you know this has never happened since the
original Constitution was drafted and subsequently ratified. Let
your legislators know that we need the voices of the people to
be heard regarding the direction the country will take. Let them
know that we all want a say in amending the Constitution and
that this responsibility should not be left up to only Congress, who
will favor changes that will benefit Congress. Ask your friends to
contact their state legislatures to take action on this issue. Let
your state legislators take the case to the state level, where your
state can coordinate with other states to achieve a united front
for a convention. The more people who contact their legislators
will make a more successful the outcome. Further, some readers
may want to organize coilitions in their individual states to lobby

their representatives to call for a states' convention for proposing amendments.

If we do nothing, nothing will result; everyone should get involved and do his or her part in this movement. We need to make Constitutional amendments that will clarify ambiguities, incorporate changes that have taken place in the structure of government, provide for a balanced budget amendment, and incorporate many other issues that are open to change. Let the government know what you want! If we start right away, we'll be on the road to a better government, a better opportunity for economic growth, and a better way of life for all of us.

With the above in mind, it seems likely that few citizens are sufficiently knowledgeable regarding what the Constitution states and how it has made provisions for making changes. The founders were well aware that changes were appropriate when identified, and certainly they already knew of some changes that would need to be amended after initial ratification. These were the Bill of Rights, and, as mentioned, they were incorporated soon after the ratification of the Constitution. In this regard we need to encourage our school systems to make the study of government an important part of their curriculums so that we're all aware of what is in the Constitution and what we can do to change the issues that need change. This should be done at the state level and in all states. States have a great influence over local school curriculums, and they should take on this responsibility. Of course it will take time for all of this to become part of our lives, particularly for those who have never taken a course in government during their school years. How can we expect people to get involved in an issue if they have no knowledge of the issue? The answer is that they will do nothing. If the people do nothing, members of Congress will continue to have the power to make all proposed amendments to the Constitution and will go forward with proposals that benefit themselves, and the country will be left in the dark.

On the Internet there have been numerous proposals presented by many different sources for people to ask their legislators to make changes that would affect the pay, perks, term limits, and other benefits provided for members of Congress during and after their Congressional terms. It's apparent that many citizens are dismayed by the benefits given to members of Congress and want to do something about it. Many individuals have proposed that we ask our legislators to propose these changes. Well, the chances of Congress approving any such changes in their benefits are slim to none and frankly will never happen. Furthermore, other proposals have gone before Congress that will never achieve approval to go forward, such as the Balanced Budget Amendment. This amendment would take power away from Congress, and as long as members of Congress are in the driver's seat, this amendment will never go forward.

There are other proposals in the same category (i.e., they will never go forward as they would diminish the power of Congress. The only way to move some of these proposals forward is by states' conventions, in which two-thirds of the states can approve a proposal and then it will go to all the states for ratification. If three-fourths ratify the proposal, it will become incorporated into the Constitution. Think about all of this. We need to get everyone involved in the amendment process, as we all count.

We must transfer some of the power of the Federal Government back to the people through the states. We must get started now. The founders fought for a limited federal government, and this is what we must do to continue the fight today. Otherwise we will find ourselves under a de facto monarchy, and it will be too late.

Let's start the movement now. Get involved!

APPENDIX I
COMPLETE TEXT OF THE
DECLARATION OF INDEPENDENCE

IN CONGRESS, JULY 4, 1776.

The unanimous Declaration of the thirteen united States of America,

When in the Course of human events, it becomes necessary for one people to dissolve the political bands which have connected them with another, and to assume among the powers of the earth, the separate and equal station to which the Laws of Nature and of Nature's God entitle them, a decent respect to the opinions of mankind requires that they should declare the causes which impel them to the separation.

We hold these truths to be self-evident, that all men are created equal, that they are endowed by their Creator with certain unalienable Rights, that among these are Life, Liberty and the pursuit of Happiness.--That to secure these rights, Governments are instituted among Men, deriving their just powers from the consent of the governed, --That whenever any Form of Government becomes destructive of these ends, it is the Right of the People to alter or to abolish it, and to institute new Government, laying its foundation on such principles and organizing its powers in such form, as to them shall seem most likely to effect their Safety and Happiness. Prudence, indeed, will dictate that Governments long established should not be changed for light and transient causes; and accordingly all experience hath shewn, that mankind are more disposed to suffer, while evils are sufferable, than to right themselves by abolishing the forms to which they are accustomed. But when a long train of abuses and usurpations, pursuing invariably the same Object evinces a design to reduce them under absolute Despotism, it is their right, it is their duty, to throw off such Government, and to provide new Guards for their future security.--Such has been the patient sufferance of these Colonies; and such is now the necessity which constrains them to alter their former Systems of Government. The history of the present King of Great Britain is a history of repeated injuries and usurpations, all having in direct object the establishment of an absolute Tyranny over these States. To prove this, let Facts be submitted to a candid world.

He has refused his Assent to Laws, the most wholesome and necessary for the public good.

He has forbidden his Governors to pass Laws of immediate and pressing importance, unless suspended in their operation till his Assent should be obtained; and when so suspended, he has utterly neglected to attend to them.

He has refused to pass other Laws for the accommodation of large districts of people, unless those people would relinquish the right of Representation in the Legislature, a right inestimable to them and formidable to tyrants only.

He has called together legislative bodies at places unusual, uncomfortable, and distant from the depository of their public Records, for the sole purpose of fatiguing them into compliance with his measures.

He has dissolved Representative Houses repeatedly, for opposing with manly firmness his invasions on the rights of the people.

He has refused for a long time, after such dissolutions, to cause others to be elected; whereby the Legislative powers, incapable of Annihilation, have returned to the People at large for their exercise; the State remaining in the mean time exposed to all the dangers of invasion from without, and convulsions within.

He has endeavoured to prevent the population of these States; for that purpose obstructing the Laws for Naturalization of Foreigners; refusing to pass others to encourage their migrations hither, and raising the conditions of new Appropriations of Lands.

He has obstructed the Administration of Justice, by refusing his Assent to Laws for establishing Judiciary powers.

He has made Judges dependent on his Will alone, for the tenure of their offices, and the amount and payment of their salaries.

He has erected a multitude of New Offices, and sent hither swarms of Officers to harrass our people, and eat out their substance.

He has kept among us, in times of peace, Standing Armies without the Consent of our legislatures.

He has affected to render the Military independent of and superior to the Civil power.

He has combined with others to subject us to a jurisdiction foreign to our constitution, and unacknowledged by our laws; giving his Assent to their Acts of pretended Legislation:

For Quartering large bodies of armed troops among us:

For protecting them, by a mock Trial, from punishment for any Murders which they should commit on the Inhabitants of these States:

For cutting off our Trade with all parts of the world:

For imposing Taxes on us without our Consent:

For depriving us in many cases, of the benefits of Trial by Jury:

For transporting us beyond Seas to be tried for pretended offences

For abolishing the free System of English Laws in a neighbouring Province, establishing therein an arbitrary government, and enlarging its Boundaries so as to render it at once an example and fit instrument for introducing the same absolute rule into these Colonies:

For taking away our Charters, abolishing our most valuable Laws, and altering fundamentally the Forms of our Governments:

For suspending our own Legislatures, and declaring themselves invested with power to legislate for us in all cases whatsoever.

He has abdicated Government here, by declaring us out of his Protection and waging War against us.

He has plundered our seas, ravaged our Coasts, burnt our towns, and destroyed the lives of our people.

He is at this time transporting large Armies of foreign Mercenaries to compleat the works of death, desolation and tyranny, already begun with circumstances of Cruelty & perfidy scarcely paralleled in the most barbarous ages, and totally unworthy the Head of a civilized nation.

He has constrained our fellow Citizens taken Captive on the high Seas to bear Arms against their Country, to become the executioners of their friends and Brethren, or to fall themselves by their Hands.

He has excited domestic insurrections amongst us, and has endeavoured to bring on the inhabitants of our frontiers, the merciless Indian Savages, whose known rule of warfare, is an undistinguished destruction of all ages, sexes and conditions.

In every stage of these Oppressions We have petitioned for Redress in the most humble terms: Our repeated Petitions have been answered only by repeated injury. A Prince whose character is thus marked by every act which may define a Tyrant, is unfit to be the ruler of a free people.

Nor have We been wanting in attention to our Brittish brethren. We have warned them from time to time of attempts by their legislature to extend an unwarrantable jurisdiction over us. We have reminded them of the circumstances of our emigration and settlement here. We have appealed to their native justice and magnanimity, and we have conjured them by the ties of our common kindred to disavow these usurpations, which, would inevitably interrupt our connections and correspondence. They too have been deaf to the voice of justice and of consanguinity. We must, therefore, acquiesce in the necessity, which denounces our Separation, and hold them, as we hold the rest of mankind, Enemies in War, in Peace Friends.

We, therefore, the Representatives of the united States of America, in General Congress, Assembled, appealing to the Supreme Judge of the world for the rectitude of our intentions, do, in the Name, and by Authority of the good People of these Colonies, solemnly publish and declare, That these United Colonies are, and of Right ought to be Free and Independent States; that they are Absolved from all Allegiance to the British Crown, and that all political connection between them and the State of Great Britain, is and ought to be totally dissolved; and that as Free and Independent States, they have full Power to levy War, conclude Peace, contract Alliances, establish Commerce, and to do all other Acts and Things which Independent States may of right do. And for the support of this Declaration, with a firm reliance on the protection of divine Providence, we mutually pledge to each other our Lives, our Fortunes and our sacred Honor.

[The fifty-six signatures on the Declaration appear in the positions indicated below.]

Column 1
Georgia:
Button Gwinnett
Lyman Hall
George Walton

Column 2
North Carolina:
William Hooper
Joseph Hewes
John Penn

South Carolina:

Edward Rutledge

Thomas Heyward, Jr.

Thomas Lynch, Jr.

Arthur Middleton

Column 3
Massachusetts:

John Hancock

Maryland:

Samuel Chase

William Paca

Thomas Stone

Charles Carroll of Carrollton

Virginia:

George Wythe

Richard Henry Lee

Thomas Jefferson

Benjamin Harrison

Thomas Nelson, Jr.

Francis Lightfoot Lee

Carter Braxton

Column 4
Pennsylvania:

Robert Morris

Benjamin Rush

Benjamin Franklin

John Morton

George Clymer

James Smith

George Taylor

James Wilson

George Ross

Delaware:

Caesar Rodney

George Read

Thomas McKean

Column 5
New York:

William Floyd

Philip Livingston

Francis Lewis

Lewis Morris

New Jersey:

Richard Stockton

John Witherspoon

Francis Hopkinson

John Hart

Abraham Clark

Column 6
New Hampshire:
Josiah Bartlett

William Whipple

Massachusetts:
Samuel Adams

John Adams

Robert Treat Paine

Elbridge Gerry

Rhode Island:
Stephen Hopkins

William Ellery

Connecticut:
Roger Sherman

Samuel Huntington

William Williams

Oliver Wolcott

New Hampshire:
Matthew Thornton

Appendix II
Complete Text of the Articles of Confederation

To all to whom these Presents shall come, we, the undersigned Delegates of the States affixed to our Names send greeting. Whereas the Delegates of the United States of America in Congress assembled did on the fifteenth day of November in the year of our Lord One Thousand Seven Hundred and Seventy seven, and in the Second Year of the Independence of America agree to certain articles of Confederation and perpetual Union between the States of Newhampshire, Massachusetts-bay, Rhodeisland and Providence Plantations, Connecticut, New York, New Jersey, Pennsylvania, Delaware, Maryland, Virginia, North Carolina, South Carolina, and Georgia in the Words following, viz. "Articles of Confederation and perpetual Union between the States of Newhampshire, Massachusetts-bay, Rhodeisland and Providence Plantations, Connecticut, New York, New Jersey, Pennsylvania, Delaware, Maryland, Virginia, North Carolina, South Carolina, and Georgia.

Article I. The Stile of this confederacy shall be, "The United States of America."

Article II. Each state retains its sovereignty, freedom and independence, and every Power, Jurisdiction and right, which is not by this confederation expressly delegated to the United States, in Congress assembled.

Article III. The said states hereby severally enter into a firm league of friendship with each other, for their common defence, the security of their Liberties, and their mutual and general welfare, binding themselves to assist each other, against all force offered to, or attacks made upon them, or any of them, on account of religion, sovereignty, trade, or any other pretence whatever.

Article IV. The better to secure and perpetuate mutual friendship and intercourse among the people of the different states in this union, the free inhabitants of each of these states, paupers, vagabonds and fugitives from Justice excepted, shall be entitled to all privileges and immunities of free citizens in the several states; and the people of each state shall have free ingress and regress to and from any other state, and shall enjoy therein all the privileges of trade and commerce, subject to the same duties, impositions and restrictions as the inhabitants thereof respectively, provided that such restrictions shall not extend so far as to prevent the removal of property imported into any state, to any other State of which the Owner is an inhabitant; provided also that no imposition, duties or restriction shall be laid by any state, on the property of the united states, or either of them.

If any Person guilty of, or charged with, treason, felony, or other high misdemeanor in any state, shall flee from Justice, and be found in any of the united states, he shall upon demand of the

Governor or executive power of the state from which he fled, be delivered up, and removed to the state having jurisdiction of his offence.

Full faith and credit shall be given in each of these states to the records, acts and judicial proceedings of the courts and magistrates of every other state.

Article V. For the more convenient management of the general interests of the united states, delegates shall be annually appointed in such manner as the legislature of each state shall direct, to meet in Congress on the first Monday in November, in every year, with a power reserved to each state to recall its delegates, or any of them, at any time within the year, and to send others in their stead, for the remainder of the Year.

No State shall be represented in Congress by less than two, nor by more than seven Members; and no person shall be capable of being delegate for more than three years, in any term of six years; nor shall any person, being a delegate, be capable of holding any office under the united states, for which he, or another for his benefit receives any salary, fees or emolument of any kind.

Each State shall maintain its own delegates in a meeting of the states, and while they act as members of the committee of the states.

In determining questions in the united states, in Congress assembled, each state shall have one vote.

Freedom of speech and debate in Congress shall not be impeached or questioned in any Court, or place out of Congress, and the members of congress shall be protected in their persons from arrests and imprisonments, during the time of their going to and from, and attendance on congress, except for treason, felony, or breach of the peace.

Article VI. No State, without the Consent of the united States, in congress assembled, shall send any embassy to, or receive any embassy from, or enter into any conferrence, agreement, alliance, or treaty, with any King prince or state; nor shall any person holding any office of profit or trust under the united states, or any of them, accept of any present, emolument, office, or title of any kind whatever, from any king, prince, or foreign state; nor shall the united states, in congress assembled, or any of them, grant any title of nobility.

No two or more states shall enter into any treaty, confederation, or alliance whatever between them, without the consent of the united states, in congress assembled, specifying accurately the purposes for which the same is to be entered into, and how long it shall continue.

No State shall lay any imposts or duties, which may interfere with any stipulations in treaties, entered into by the united States in congress assembled, with any king, prince, or State, in pursuance of any treaties already proposed by congress, to the courts of France and Spain.

No vessels of war shall be kept up in time of peace, by any state, except such number only, as shall be deemed necessary by the united states, in congress assembled, for the defence of such state, or its trade; nor shall any body of forces be kept up, by any state, in time of peace, except such number only as, in the judgment of the united states, in congress assembled, shall be deemed requisite to garrison the forts necessary for the defence of such state; but every state shall always keep up a well regulated and disciplined militia, sufficiently armed and accounted, and shall provide and constantly have ready for use, in public stores, a due number of field pieces and tents, and a proper quantity of arms, ammunition, and camp equipage.

No State shall engage in any war without the consent of the united States in congress assembled, unless such State be actually invaded by enemies, or shall have received certain advice of a resolution being formed by some nation of Indians to invade such State, and the danger is so imminent as not to admit of a delay till the united states in congress assembled, can be consulted: nor shall any state grant commissions to any ships or vessels of war, nor letters of marque or reprisal, except it be after a declaration of war by the united states in congress assembled, and then only against the kingdom or State, and the subjects thereof, against which war has been so declared, and under such regulations as shall be established by the united states in congress assembled, unless such state be infested by pirates, in which case vessels of war may be fitted out for that occasion, and kept so long as the danger shall continue, or until the united states in congress assembled shall determine otherwise.

Article VII. When land forces are raised by any state, for the common defence, all officers of or under the rank of colonel, shall be appointed by the legislature of each state respectively by whom such forces shall be raised, or in such manner as such state shall direct, and all vacancies shall be filled up by the state which first made appointment.

Article VIII. All charges of war, and all other expenses that shall be incurred for the common defence or general welfare, and allowed by the united states in congress assembled, shall be defrayed out of a common treasury, which shall be supplied by the several states, in proportion to the value of all land within each state, granted to or surveyed for any Person, as such land and the buildings and improvements thereon shall be estimated, according to such mode as the united states, in congress assembled, shall, from time to time, direct and appoint. The taxes for paying that proportion shall be laid and levied by the authority and direction of the legislatures of the several states within the time agreed upon by the united states in congress assembled.

Article IX. The united states, in congress assembled, shall have the sole and exclusive right and power of determining on peace and war, except in the cases mentioned in the sixth article - of sending and receiving ambassadors - entering into treaties and alliances, provided that no treaty of commerce shall be made, whereby the legislative power of the respective states shall be restrained from imposing such imposts and duties on foreigners, as their own people are subjected to, or from prohibiting the exportation or importation of any species of goods or commodities whatsoever - of establishing rules for deciding, in all cases, what captures on land or water shall be legal, and in what manner prizes taken by land or naval forces in the service of the united Sates, shall be divided or appropriated - of granting letters of marque and reprisal in times of peace - appointing courts for the trial of piracies and felonies committed on the high seas; and establishing courts; for receiving and determining finally appeals in all cases of captures; provided that no member of congress shall be appointed a judge of any of the said courts.

The united states, in congress assembled, shall also be the last resort on appeal, in all disputes and differences now subsisting, or that hereafter may arise between two or more states concerning boundary, jurisdiction, or any other cause whatever; which authority shall always be exercised in the manner following. Whenever the legislative or executive authority, or lawful agent of any state in controversy with another, shall present a petition to congress, stating the matter in question, and praying for a hearing, notice thereof shall be given, by order of congress, to the legislative or executive authority of the other state in controversy, and a day assigned for the appearance of the parties by their lawful agents, who shall then be directed to appoint, by joint consent, commissioners or judges to constitute a court for hearing and determining the matter in question: but if they cannot agree, congress shall name three persons out of each of the united states, and from the list of such persons each party shall alternately strike out one, the petitioners beginning, until the number shall be reduced to thirteen; and from that number not less than seven, nor more than nine names, as congress shall direct, shall, in the presence of congress, be drawn out by lot, and the persons whose names shall be so drawn, or any five of them, shall be commissioners or judges, to hear and finally determine the controversy, so always as a major part of the judges, who shall hear the cause, shall agree in the determination: and if either party shall neglect to attend at the day appointed, without showing reasons which congress shall judge sufficient, or being present, shall refuse to strike, the congress shall proceed to nominate three persons out of each State, and the secretary of congress shall strike in behalf of such party absent or refusing; and the judgment and sentence of the court, to be appointed in the manner before prescribed, shall be final and conclusive; and if any of the parties shall refuse to submit to the authority of such court, or to appear or defend their claim or cause, the court shall nevertheless proceed to pronounce sentence, or judgment, which shall in like manner be final and decisive; the judgment or sentence and other proceedings being in either case transmitted to congress, and lodged among the acts of congress, for the security of the parties concerned: provided that every commissioner, before he sits in judgment, shall take an oath to be administered by one of the judges of the supreme or superior court of the State where the cause shall be tried, "well and truly to hear and determine the matter in question, according to the best of his judgment, without favour, affection, or hope of reward: "provided, also, that no State shall be deprived of territory for the benefit of the united states.

All controversies concerning the private right of soil claimed under different grants of two or more states, whose jurisdictions as they may respect such lands, and the states which passed such grants are adjusted, the said grants or either of them being at the same time claimed to have originated antecedent to such settlement of jurisdiction, shall, on the petition of either party to the congress of the united states, be finally determined, as near as may be, in the same manner as is before prescribed for deciding disputes respecting territorial jurisdiction between different states.

The united states, in congress assembled, shall also have the sole and exclusive right and power of regulating the alloy and value of coin struck by their own authority, or by that of the respective states - fixing the standard of weights and measures throughout the united states - regulating the trade and managing all affairs with the Indians, not members of any of the states; provided that the legislative right of any state, within its own limits, be not infringed or violated - establishing and regulating post-offices from one state to another, throughout all the united states, and exacting such postage on the papers passing through the same, as may be requisite to defray the expenses of the said office - appointing all officers of the land forces in the service of the united States, excepting regimental officers - appointing all the officers of the naval forces, and commissioning all officers whatever in the service of the united states; making rules for the government and regulation of the said land and naval forces, and directing their operations.

The united States, in congress assembled, shall have authority to appoint a committee, to sit in the recess of congress, to be denominated, "A Committee of the States," and to consist of one delegate from each State; and to appoint such other committees and civil officers as may be necessary for managing the general affairs of the united states under their direction - to appoint one of their number to preside; provided that no person be allowed to serve in the office of president more than one year in any term of three years; to ascertain the necessary sums of money to be raised for the service of the united states, and to appropriate and apply the same for defraying the public expenses; to borrow money or emit bills on the credit of the united states, transmitting every half year to the respective states an account of the sums of money so borrowed or emitted, - to build and equip a navy - to agree upon the number of land forces, and to make requisitions from each state for its quota, in proportion to the number of white inhabitants in such state, which requisition shall be binding; and thereupon the legislature of each state shall appoint the regimental officers, raise the men, and clothe, arm, and equip them, in a soldier-like manner, at the expense of the united states; and the officers and men so clothed, armed, and equipped, shall march to the place appointed, and within the time agreed on by the united states, in congress assembled; but if the united states, in congress assembled, shall, on consideration of circumstances, judge proper that any state should not raise men, or should raise a smaller number than its quota, and that any other state should raise a greater number of men than the quota thereof, such extra number shall be raised, officered, clothed, armed, and equipped in the same manner as the quota of such state, unless the legislature of such state shall judge that such extra number cannot be safely spared out of the same, in which case they shall raise, officer, clothe, arm, and equip, as many of such extra number as they judge can be safely spared. And the officers and men so clothed, armed, and equipped, shall march to the place appointed, and within the time agreed on by the united states in congress assembled.

The united states, in congress assembled, shall never engage in a war, nor grant letters of marque and reprisal in time of peace, nor enter into any treaties or alliances, nor coin money, nor regulate the value thereof nor ascertain the sums and expenses necessary for the defence and welfare of the united states, or any of them, nor emit bills, nor borrow money on the credit of the united states, nor appropriate money, nor agree upon the number of vessels of war to be built or purchased, or the number of land or sea forces to be raised, nor appoint a commander in chief of the army or navy, unless nine states assent to the same, nor shall a question on any other point, except for adjourning from day to day, be determined, unless by the votes of a majority of the united states in congress assembled.

The congress of the united states shall have power to adjourn to any time within the year, and to any place within the united states, so that no period of adjournment be for a longer duration than the space of six Months, and shall publish the Journal of their proceedings monthly, except such parts thereof relating to treaties, alliances, or military operations, as in their judgment require secrecy; and the yeas and nays of the delegates of each State, on any question, shall be entered on the Journal, when it is desired by any delegate; and the delegates of a State, or any of them, at his or their request, shall be furnished with a transcript of the said Journal, except such parts as are above excepted, to lay before the legislatures of the several states.

Article X. The committee of the states, or any nine of them, shall be authorized to execute, in the recess of congress, such of the powers of congress as the united states, in congress assembled, by the consent of nine states, shall, from time to time, think expedient to vest them with; provided that no power be delegated to the said committee, for the exercise of which, by the articles of confederation, the voice of nine states, in the congress of the united states assembled, is requisite.

Article XI. Canada acceding to this confederation, and joining in the measures of the united states, shall be admitted into, and entitled to all the advantages of this union: but no other colony shall be admitted into the same, unless such admission be agreed to by nine states.

Article XII. All bills of credit emitted, monies borrowed, and debts contracted by or under the authority of congress, before the assembling of the united states, in pursuance of the present confederation, shall be deemed and considered as a charge against the united States, for payment and satisfaction whereof the said united states and the public faith are hereby solemnly pledged.

Article XIII. Every State shall abide by the determinations of the united states, in congress assembled, on all questions which by this confederation are submitted to them. And the Articles of this confederation shall be inviolably observed by every state, and the union shall be perpetual; nor shall any alteration at any time hereafter be made in any of them, unless such alteration be agreed to in a congress of the united states, and be afterwards con-firmed by the legislatures of every state.

And Whereas it hath pleased the Great Governor of the World to incline the hearts of the legislatures we respectively represent in congress, to approve of, and to authorize us to ratify the said articles of confederation and perpetual union, Know Ye, that we, the undersigned delegates, by virtue of the power and authority to us given for that purpose, do, by these presents, in the name and in behalf of our respective constituents, fully and entirely ratify and confirm each and every of the said articles of confederation and perpetual union, and all and singular the matters and things therein contained. And we do further solemnly plight and engage the faith of our respective constituents, that they shall abide by the determinations of the united states in congress assembled, on all questions, which by the said confederation are submitted to them. And that the articles thereof shall be inviolably observed by the states we respectively represent, and that the union shall be perpetual. In Witness whereof, we have hereunto set our hands, in Congress. Done at Philadelphia, in the State of Pennsylvania, the ninth Day of July, in the Year of our Lord one Thousand seven Hundred and Seventy eight, and in the third year of the Independence of America.

APPENDIX III
COMPLETE TEXT OF THE CONSTITUTION OF
THE UNITED STATES OF AMERICA

We the People of the United States, in Order to form a more perfect Union, establish Justice, insure domestic Tranquility, provide for the common defence, promote the general Welfare, and secure the Blessings of Liberty to ourselves and our Posterity, do ordain and establish this Constitution for the United States of America.

ARTICLE I
SECTION 1
All legislative Powers herein granted shall be vested in a Congress of the United States, which shall consist of a Senate and House of Representatives.

SECTION 2
The House of Representatives shall be composed of Members chosen every second Year by the People of the several States, and the Electors in each State shall have the Qualifications

requisite for Electors of the most numerous Branch of the State Legislature.

No Person shall be a Representative who shall not have attained to the Age of twenty five Years, and been seven Years a Citizen of the United States, and who shall not, when elected, be an Inhabitant of that State in which he shall be chosen.

Representatives and direct Taxes shall be apportioned among the several States which may be included within this Union, according to their respective Numbers, which shall be determined by adding to the whole Number of free Persons, including those bound to Service for a Term of Years, and excluding Indians not taxed, three fifths of all other Persons. The actual Enumeration shall be made within three Years after the first Meeting of the Congress of the United States, and within every subsequent Term of ten Years, in such Manner as they shall by Law direct.

The Number of Representatives shall not exceed one for every thirty Thousand, but each State shall have at Least one Representative; and until such enumeration shall be made, the State of New Hampshire shall be entitled to chuse three, Massachusetts eight, Rhode-Island and Providence Plantations one, Connecticut five, New-York six, New Jersey four, Pennsylvania eight, Delaware one, Maryland six, Virginia ten, North Carolina five, South Carolina five, and Georgia three.

When vacancies happen in the Representation from any State, the Executive Authority thereof shall issue Writs of Election to fill such Vacancies. The House of Representatives shall chuse their Speaker and other Officers; and shall have the sole Power of Impeachment.

SECTION 3

The Senate of the United States shall be composed of two Senators from each State, chosen by the Legislature thereof, for six Years; and each Senator shall have one Vote.

Immediately after they shall be assembled in Consequence of the first Election, they shall be divided as equally as may be into three Classes. The Seats of the Senators of the first Class shall be vacated at the Expiration of the second Year, of the second Class at the Expiration of the fourth Year, and of the third Class at the Expiration of the sixth Year, so that one third may be chosen every second Year; and if Vacancies happen by Resignation, or otherwise, during the Recess of the Legislature of any State, the Executive thereof may make temporary Appointments until the next Meeting of the Legislature, which shall then fill such Vacancies.

No Person shall be a Senator who shall not have attained to the Age of thirty Years, and been nine Years a Citizen of the United States, and who shall not, when elected, be an Inhabitant of that State for which he shall be chosen.
The Vice President of the United States shall be President of the Senate, but shall have no Vote, unless they be equally divided.

The Senate shall chuse their other Officers, and also a President pro tempore, in the Absence of the Vice President, or when he shall exercise the Office of President of the United States.

The Senate shall have the sole Power to try all Impeachments. When sitting for that Purpose, they shall be on Oath or Affirmation. When the President of the United States is tried, the Chief Justice shall preside: And no Person shall be convicted without the Concurrence of two thirds of the Members present.

Judgment in Cases of Impeachment shall not extend further than to removal from Office, and disqualification to hold and enjoy any Office of honor, Trust or Profit under the United States: but the Party convicted shall nevertheless be liable and subject to Indictment, Trial, Judgment and Punishment, according to Law.

SECTION 4

The Times, Places and Manner of holding Elections for Senators and Representatives, shall be prescribed in each State by the Legislature thereof; but the Congress may at any time by Law make or alter such Regulations, except as to the Places of chusing Senators.

The Congress shall assemble at least once in every Year, and such Meeting shall be on the first Monday in December, unless they shall by Law appoint a different Day.

SECTION 5

Each House shall be the Judge of the Elections, Returns and Qualifications of its own Members, and a Majority of each shall constitute a Quorum to do Business; but a smaller Number may adjourn from day to day, and may be authorized to compel the Attendance of absent Members, in such Manner, and under such Penalties as each House may provide.

Each House may determine the Rules of its Proceedings, punish its Members for disorderly Behaviour, and, with the Concurrence of two thirds, expel a Member.

Each House shall keep a Journal of its Proceedings, and from time to time publish the same, excepting such Parts as may in their Judgment require Secrecy; and the Yeas and Nays of the Members of either House on any question shall, at the Desire of one fifth of those Present, be entered on the Journal.

Neither House, during the Session of Congress, shall, without the Consent of the other, adjourn for more than three days, nor to any other Place than that in which the two Houses shall be sitting.

SECTION 6

The Senators and Representatives shall receive a Compensation for their Services, to be ascertained by Law, and paid out of the Treasury of the United States. They shall in all Cases, except Treason, Felony and Breach of the Peace, be privileged from Arrest during their Attendance at the Session of their respective Houses, and in going to and returning from the same; and for any

Speech or Debate in either House, they shall not be questioned in any other Place.

No Senator or Representative shall, during the Time for which he was elected, be appointed to any civil Office under the Authority of the United States, which shall have been created, or the Emoluments whereof shall have been encreased during such time; and no Person holding any Office under the United States, shall be a Member of either House during his Continuance in Office.

SECTION 7

All Bills for raising Revenue shall originate in the House of Representatives; but the Senate may propose or concur with Amendments as on other Bills.

Every Bill which shall have passed the House of Representatives and the Senate, shall, before it become a Law, be presented to the President of the United States; If he approve he shall sign it, but if not he shall return it, with his Objections to that House in which it shall have originated, who shall enter the Objections at large on their Journal, and proceed to reconsider it. If after such Reconsideration two thirds of that House shall agree to pass the Bill, it shall be sent, together with the Objections, to the other House, by which it shall likewise be reconsidered, and if approved by two thirds of that House, it shall become a Law. But in all such Cases the Votes of both Houses shall be determined by Yeas and Nays, and the Names of the Persons voting for and against the Bill shall be entered on the Journal of each House respectively, If any Bill shall not be returned by the President within ten Days (Sundays excepted) after it shall have been presented to him, the

Same shall be a Law, in like Manner as if he had signed it, unless the Congress by their Adjournment prevent its Return, in which Case it shall not be a Law.

Every Order, Resolution, or Vote to which the Concurrence of the Senate and House of Representatives may be necessary (except on a question of Adjournment) shall be presented to the President of the United States; and before the Same shall take Effect, shall be approved by him, or being disapproved by him, shall be repassed by two thirds of the Senate and House of Representatives, according to the Rules and Limitations prescribed in the Case of a Bill.

SECTION 8

The Congress shall have Power To lay and collect Taxes, Duties, Imposts and Excises, to pay the Debts and provide for the common Defence and general Welfare of the United States; but all Duties, Imposts and Excises shall be uniform throughout the United States;

To borrow Money on the credit of the United States;

To regulate Commerce with foreign Nations, and among the several States, and with the Indian Tribes;

To establish an uniform Rule of Naturalization, and uniform Laws on the subject of Bankruptcies throughout the United States;

To coin Money, regulate the Value thereof, and of foreign Coin, and fix the Standard of Weights and Measures;

To provide for the Punishment of counterfeiting the Securities and current Coin of the United States;

To establish Post Offices and post Roads;

To promote the Progress of Science and useful Arts, by securing for limited Times to Authors and Inventors the exclusive Right to their respective Writings and Discoveries;

To constitute Tribunals inferior to the supreme Court;

To define and punish Piracies and Felonies committed on the high Seas, and Offenses against the Law of Nations;

To declare War, grant Letters of Marque and Reprisal, and make Rules concerning Captures on Land and Water;

To raise and support Armies, but no Appropriation of Money to that Use shall be for a longer Term than two Years;

To provide and maintain a Navy;

To make Rules for the Government and Regulation of the land and naval Forces;

To provide for calling forth the Militia to execute the Laws of the Union, suppress Insurrections and repel Invasions;

To provide for organizing, arming, and disciplining, the Militia, and for governing such Part of them as may be employed in the Service of the United States, reserving to the States respectively, the Appointment of the Officers, and the Authority of training the Militia according to the discipline prescribed by Congress;

To exercise exclusive Legislation in all Cases whatsoever, over such District (not exceeding ten Miles square) as may, by Cession of particular States, and the Acceptance of Congress, become the Seat of the Government of the United States, and to exercise like Authority over all Places purchased by the Consent of the Legislature of the State in which the Same shall be, for the Erection of Forts, Magazines, Arsenals, dock-Yards and other needful Buildings;-And

To make all Laws which shall be necessary and proper for carrying into Execution the foregoing Powers, and all other Powers vested by this Constitution in the Government of the United States, or in any Department or Officer thereof.

SECTION 9

The Migration or Importation of such Persons as any of the States now existing shall think proper to admit, shall not be prohibited by the Congress prior to the Year one thousand eight hundred and eight, but a Tax or duty may be imposed on such Importation, not exceeding ten dollars for each Person.

The Privilege of the Writ of Habeas Corpus shall not be suspended, unless when in Cases of Rebellion or Invasion the public Safety may require it.

No Bill of Attainder or ex post facto Law shall be passed.

No Capitation, or other direct, Tax shall be laid, unless in Proportion to the Census or Enumeration herein before directed to be taken.

No Tax or Duty shall be laid on Articles exported from any State.

No Preference shall be given by any Regulation of Commerce or Revenue to the Ports of one State over those of another: nor shall Vessels bound to, or from, one State, be obliged to enter, clear, or pay Duties in another.

No Money shall be drawn from the Treasury, but in Consequence of Appropriations made by Law; and a regular Statement and Account of the Receipts and Expenditures of all public Money shall be published from time to time.

No Title of Nobility shall be granted by the United States: And no Person holding any Office of Profit or Trust under them, shall, without the Consent of the Congress, accept of any present, Emolument, Office, or Title, of any kind whatever, from any King, Prince, or foreign State.

SECTION 10

No State shall enter into any Treaty, Alliance, or Confederation; grant Letters of Marque and Reprisal; coin Money; emit Bills of Credit; make any Thing but gold and silver Coin a Tender in Payment of Debts; pass any Bill of Attainder, ex post facto Law, or Law impairing the Obligation of Contracts, or grant any Title of Nobility.

No State shall, without the Consent of the Congress, lay any Imposts or Duties on Imports or Exports, except what may be absolutely necessary for executing it's inspection Laws: and the net Produce of all Duties and Imposts, laid by any State on Imports or Exports, shall be for the Use of the Treasury of the United States; and all such Laws shall be subject to the Revision and Controul of the Congress.

No State shall, without the Consent of Congress, lay any Duty of Tonnage, keep Troops, or Ships of War in time of Peace, enter into any Agreement or Compact with another

State, or with a foreign Power, or engage in War, unless actually invaded, or in such imminent Danger as will not admit of delay.

ARTICLE II
SECTION 1

The executive Power shall be vested in a President of the United States of America. He shall hold his Office during the Term of four Years, and, together with the Vice President, chosen for the same Term, be elected, as follows:

Each State shall appoint, in such Manner as the Legislature thereof may direct, a Number of Electors, equal to the whole Number of Senators and Representatives to which the State may be entitled in the Congress: but no Senator or Representative, or Person holding an Office of Trust or Profit under the United States, shall be appointed an Elector.

The Electors shall meet in their respective States, and vote by Ballot for two Persons, of whom one at least shall not be an Inhabitant of the same State with themselves. And they shall make a List of all the Persons voted for, and of the Number of Votes for each; which List they shall sign and certify, and transmit sealed to the Seat of the Government of the United States, directed to the President of the Senate.

The President of the Senate shall, in the Presence of the Senate and House of Representatives, open all the Certificates, and the Votes shall then be counted. The Person having the greatest Number of Votes shall be the President, if such Number be a Majority of the whole Number of Electors appointed; and if there be more than one who have such Majority, and have an equal Number of Votes, then the House of Representatives shall immediately chuse by Ballot one of them for President; and if no Person have a Majority, then from the five highest on the List the said House shall in like Manner chuse the President. But in chusing the President, the Votes shall be taken by States, the Representation from each State having one Vote; a quorum for this Purpose shall consist of a Member or Members from two thirds of the States, and a Majority of all the States shall be necessary to a Choice.

In every Case, after the Choice of the President, the Person having the greatest Number of Votes of the Electors shall be the Vice President. But if there should remain two or more who have equal Votes, the Senate shall chuse from them by Ballot the Vice President.

The Congress may determine the Time of chusing the Electors, and the Day on which they shall give their Votes; which Day shall be the same throughout the United States.

No Person except a natural born Citizen, or a Citizen of the United States, at the time of the Adoption of this Constitution, shall be eligible to the Office of President; neither shall any person be eligible to that Office who shall not have attained to the Age of thirty five Years, and been fourteen Years a Resident within the United States.

In Case of the Removal of the President from Office, or of his Death, Resignation, or Inability to discharge the Powers and Duties of the said Office, the Same shall devolve on the Vice President, and the Congress may by Law provide for the Case of Removal, Death, Resignation or Inability, both of the President and Vice President, declaring what Officer shall then act as President, and such Officer shall act accordingly, until the Disability be removed, or a President shall be elected.

The President shall, at Stated Times, receive for his Services, a Compensation, which shall neither be increased nor diminished during the Period for which he shall have been elected, and he shall not receive within that Period any other Emolument from the United States, or any of them.

Before he enter on the Execution of his Office, he shall take the following Oath or Affirmation:--"I do solemnly swear (or affirm) that I will faithfully execute the Office of President of the United States, and will to the best of my Ability, preserve, protect and defend the Constitution of the United States."

SECTION 2

The President shall be Commander in Chief of the Army and Navy of the United States, and of the Militia of the several States, when called into the actual Service of the United States; he may require the Opinion, in writing, of the principal Officer in each of the executive Departments, upon any Subject relating to the Duties of their respective Offices, and he shall have Power to grant Reprieves and Pardons for Offenses against the United States, except in Cases of Impeachment.

He shall have Power, by and with the Advice and Consent of the Senate, to make Treaties, provided two thirds of the Senators present concur; and he shall nominate, and by and with the Advice and Consent of the Senate, shall appoint Ambassadors, other public Ministers and Consuls, Judges of the supreme Court, and all other Officers of the United States, whose Appointments are not herein otherwise provided for, and which shall be established by Law: but the Congress may by Law vest the Appointment of such inferior Officers, as they think proper, in the President alone, in the Courts of Law, or in the Heads of Departments.

The President shall have Power to fill up all Vacancies that may happen during the Recess of the Senate, by granting Commissions which shall expire at the End of their next Session.

SECTION 3

He shall from time to time give to the Congress Information of the State of the Union, and recommend to their Consideration such Measures as he shall judge necessary and expedient; he may, on extraordinary Occasions, convene both Houses, or either of them, and in Case of Disagreement between them, with Respect to the Time of Adjournment, he may adjourn them to such Time as he shall think proper; he shall receive Ambassadors and other public Ministers; he shall take Care that the Laws be faithfully executed, and shall Commission all the Officers of the United States.

SECTION 4

The President, Vice President and all civil Officers of the United States, shall be removed from Office on Impeachment for, and Conviction of, Treason, Bribery, or other high Crimes and Misdemeanors.

ARTICLE III
SECTION 1

The judicial Power of the United States shall be vested in one supreme Court, and in such inferior Courts as the Congress may from time to time ordain and establish. The Judges, both of the supreme and inferior Courts, shall hold their Offices during good Behaviour, and shall at Stated Times, receive for their Services, a Compensation, which shall not be diminished during their Continuance in Office.

SECTION 2

The judicial Power shall extend to all Cases, in Law and Equity, arising under this Constitution, the Laws of the United States, and Treaties made, or which shall be made, under their Authority;—to all Cases affecting Ambassadors, other public Ministers and Consuls;—to all Cases of admiralty and maritime Jurisdiction;—to Controversies to which the United States shall be a Party;—to Controversies between two or more States;—between a State and Citizens of another State,—between Citizens of different States,—between Citizens of the same State claiming Lands under Grants of different States, and between a State, or the Citizens thereof, and foreign States, Citizens or Subjects.

In all Cases affecting Ambassadors, other public Ministers and Consuls, and those in which a State shall be Party, the supreme Court shall have original Jurisdiction. In all the other Cases before mentioned, the supreme Court shall have appellate Jurisdiction, both as to Law and Fact, with such Exceptions, and under such Regulations as the Congress shall make.

The Trial of all Crimes, except in Cases of Impeachment; shall be by Jury; and such Trial shall be held in the State where the said Crimes shall have been committed; but when not committed within any State, the Trial shall be at such Place or Places as the Congress may by Law have directed.

SECTION 3

Treason against the United States, shall consist only in levying War against them, or in adhering to their Enemies, giving them Aid and Comfort. No Person shall be convicted of Treason unless on the Testimony of two Witnesses to the same overt Act, or on Confession in open Court.

The Congress shall have Power to declare the Punishment of Treason, but no Attainder of Treason shall work Corruption of Blood, or Forfeiture except during the Life of the Person attainted.

ARTICLE IV

SECTION 1

Full Faith and Credit shall be given in each State to the public Acts, Records, and judicial Proceedings of every other State. And the Congress may by general Laws prescribe the Manner in which such Acts, Records and Proceedings shall be proved, and the Effect thereof.

SECTION 2

The Citizens of each State shall be entitled to all Privileges and Immunities of Citizens in the several States.

A Person charged in any State with Treason, Felony, or other Crime, who shall flee from Justice, and be found in another State, shall on Demand of the executive Authority of the State from which he fled, be delivered up, to be removed to the State having Jurisdiction of the Crime.

No Person held to Service or Labour in one State, under the Laws thereof, escaping into another, shall, in Consequence of any Law or Regulation therein, be discharged from such Service or Labour, but shall be delivered up on Claim of the Party to whom such Service or Labour may be due.

SECTION 3

New States may be admitted by the Congress into this Union; but no new State shall be formed or erected within the Jurisdiction of any other State; nor any State be formed by the Junction of two or more States, or Parts of States, without the Consent of the Legislatures of the States concerned as well as of the Congress.

The Congress shall have Power to dispose of and make all needful Rules and Regulations respecting the Territory or other Property belonging to the United States; and nothing in this Constitution shall be so construed as to Prejudice any Claims of the United States, or of any particular State.

SECTION 4
The United States shall guarantee to every State in this Union a Republican Form of Government, and shall protect each of them against Invasion; and on Application of the Legislature, or of the Executive (when the Legislature cannot be convened) against domestic Violence.

ARTICLE V
The Congress, whenever two thirds of both Houses shall deem it necessary, shall propose Amendments to this Constitution, or, on the Application of the Legislatures of two thirds of the several States, shall call a Convention for proposing Amendments, which in either Case, shall be valid to all Intents and Purposes, as Part of this Constitution, when ratified by the Legislatures of three-fourths of the several States, or by Conventions in three fourths thereof, as the one or the other Mode of Ratification may be proposed by the Congress; Provided that no Amendment which may be made prior to the Year One thousand

eight hundred and eight shall in any Manner affect the first and fourth Clauses in the Ninth Section of the first Article; and that no State, without its Consent, shall be deprived of its equal Suffrage in the Senate.

ARTICLE VI

All Debts contracted and Engagements entered into, before the Adoption of this Constitution, shall be as valid against the United States under this Constitution, as under the Confederation.

This Constitution, and the Laws of the United States which shall be made in Pursuance thereof; and all Treaties made, or which shall be made, under the Authority of the United States, shall be the supreme Law of the Land; and the Judges in every State shall be bound thereby, any Thing in the Constitution or Laws of any State to the Contrary notwithstanding.

The Senators and Representatives before mentioned, and the Members of the several State Legislatures, and all executive and judicial Officers, both of the United States and of the several States, shall be bound by Oath or Affirmation, to support this Constitution; but no religious Test shall ever be required as a Qualification to any Office or public Trust under the United States.

ARTICLE VII

The Ratification of the Conventions of nine States, shall be sufficient for the Establishment of this Constitution between the States so ratifying the Same.

The Word, "the," being interlined between the seventh and eighth Lines of the first Page, the Word "Thirty" being partly written on an Erazure in the fifteenth Line of the first Page, The Words "is tried" being interlined between the thirty second and thirty third Lines of the first Page and the Word "the" being interlined between the forty third and forty fourth Lines of the second Page.

Attest William Jackson Secretary

Done in Convention by the Unanimous Consent of the States present the Seventeenth Day of September in the Year of our Lord one thousand seven hundred and Eighty seven and of the Independence of the United States of America the Twelfth In Witness whereof We have hereunto subscribed our Names,

Go. Washington
Presidt and deputy from Virginia

NEW HAMPSHIRE
John Langdon
Nicholas Gilman

MASSACHUSETTS
Nathaniel Gorham
Rufus King

CONNECTICUT
Wm. Saml. Johnson
Roger Sherman

NEW YORK
Alexander Hamilton

NEW JERSEY
Wil: Livingston
David Brearley
Wm. Paterson
Jona: Dayton

PENNSYLVANIA
B Franklin
Thomas Mifflin
Robt Morris
Geo. Clymer
Thos. FitzSimons
Jared Ingersoll
James Wilson
Gouv Morris

DELAWARE
Geo: Read
Gunning Bedford jun
John Dickinson
Richard Bassett
Jaco: Broom

MARYLAND
James McHenry
Dan of St Thos. Jenifer
Danl. Carroll

VIRGINIA
John Blair
James Madison Jr.

NORTH CAROLINA
Wm. Blount
Richd. Dobbs Spaight
Hu Williamson

SOUTH CAROLINA
J. Rutledge
Charles Cotesworth Pinckney
Charles Pinckney
Pierce Butler

GEORGIA
William Few
Abr Baldwin

APPENDIX IV
THE TWENTY-SEVEN AMENDMENTS
TO THE US CONSTITUTION

AMENDMENT I

Congress shall make no law respecting an establishment of religion, or prohibiting the free exercise thereof; or abridging the freedom of speech, or of the press, or the right of the people peaceably to assemble, and to petition the Government for a redress of grievances.

AMENDMENT II

A well regulated Militia, being necessary to the security of a free State, the right of the people to keep and bear Arms, shall not be infringed.

AMENDMENT III

No Soldier shall, in time of peace be quartered in any house, without the consent of the Owner, nor in time of war, but in a manner to be prescribed by law.

AMENDMENT IV

The right of the people to be secure in their persons, houses, papers, and effects, against unreasonable searches and seizures, shall not be violated, and no Warrants shall issue, but upon probable cause, supported by Oath or affirmation, and particularly describing the place to be searched, and the persons or things to be seized.

AMENDMENT V

No person shall be held to answer for a capital, or otherwise infamous crime, unless on a presentment or indictment of a Grand Jury, except in cases arising in the land or naval forces, or in the Militia, when in actual service in time of War or public danger; nor shall any person be subject for the same offence to be twice put in jeopardy of life or limb; nor shall be compelled in any criminal case to be a witness against himself, nor be deprived of life, liberty, or property, without due process of law; nor shall private property be taken for public use, without just compensation.

AMENDMENT VI

In all criminal prosecutions, the accused shall enjoy the right to a speedy and public trial, by an impartial jury of the State and district wherein the crime shall have been committed, which district shall have been previously ascertained by law, and to be informed of the nature and cause of the accusation; to be confronted with the witnesses against him; to have compulsory process for obtaining witnesses in his favor, and to have the Assistance of Counsel for his defence.

AMENDMENT VII

In suits at common law, where the value in controversy shall exceed twenty dollars, the right of trial by jury shall be preserved, and no fact tried by a jury shall be otherwise reexamined in any Court of the United States, than according to the rules of the common law.

AMENDMENT VIII

Excessive bail shall not be required, nor excessive fines imposed, nor cruel and unusual punishments inflicted.

AMENDMENT IX

The enumeration in the Constitution, of certain rights, shall not be construed to deny or disparage others retained by the people.

AMENDMENT X

The powers not delegated to the United States by the Constitution, nor prohibited by it to the States, are reserved to the States respectively, or to the people.

AMENDMENT XI

Passed by Congress March 4, 1794; ratified February 7, 1795.
The Judicial power of the United States shall not be construed to extend to any suit in law or equity, commenced or prosecuted against one of the United States by Citizens of another State, or by Citizens or Subjects of any Foreign State.

AMENDMENT XII

Passed by Congress December 9, 1803; ratified June 15, 1804.

The Electors shall meet in their respective States, and vote by ballot for President and Vice-President, one of whom, at least, shall not be an inhabitant of the same State with themselves; they shall name in their ballots the person voted for as President, and in distinct ballots the person vote for as Vice-President, and they shall make distinct lists of all persons voted for as President, and of all persons voted for as Vice-President, and of the number of votes for each, which lists they shall sign and certify, and transmit sealed to the seat of the government of the United States, directed to the President of the Senate;—the President of the Senate shall, in the presence of the Senate and House of Representatives, open all the certificates and the votes shall then be counted;-The person having the greatest number of votes for President, shall be the President, if such number be a majority of the whole number of Electors appointed; and if no person have such majority, then from the persons having the highest numbers not exceeding three on the list of those voted for as President, the House of Representatives shall choose immediately, by ballot, the President. But in choosing the President, the votes shall be taken by States, the representation from each State having one vote; a quorum for this purpose shall consist of a member or members from two-thirds of the States, and a majority of all the States shall be necessary to a choice. And if the House of Representatives

shall not choose a President whenever the right of choice shall devolve upon them, before the fourth day of March next following, then the Vice-President shall act as President, as in case of the death or other constitutional disability of the President.—]*
The person having the greatest number of votes as Vice-President, shall be the Vice-President, if such number be a majority of the whole number of Electors appointed, and if no person have a majority, then from the two highest numbers on the list, the Senate shall choose the Vice-President; a quorum for the purpose shall consist of two-thirds of the whole number of Senators, and a majority of the whole number shall be necessary to a choice. But no person constitutionally ineligible to the office of President shall be eligible to that of Vice-President of the United States.

Superseded by Section 3 of the Twentieth Amendment.

AMENDMENT XIII

Passed by Congress January 31, 1865; ratified December 6, 1865.

SECTION 1

Neither slavery nor involuntary servitude, except as a punishment for crime whereof the party shall have been duly convicted, shall exist within the United States, or any place subject to their jurisdiction.

SECTION 2

Congress shall have power to enforce this article by appropriate legislation.

AMENDMENT XIV

Passed by Congress June 13, 1866; ratified July 9, 1868.

SECTION 1

All persons born or naturalized in the United States, and subject to the jurisdiction thereof, are citizens of the United States and of the State wherein they reside. No State shall make or enforce any law which shall abridge the privileges or immunities of citizens of the United States; nor shall any State deprive any person of life, liberty, or property, without due process of law; nor deny to any person within its jurisdiction the equal protection of the laws.

SECTION 2

Representatives shall be apportioned among the several States according to their respective numbers, counting the whole number of persons in each State, excluding Indians not taxed. But when the right to vote at any election for the choice of electors for President and Vice President of the United States, Representatives in Congress, the Executive and Judicial officers of a State, or the members of the Legislature thereof, is denied to any of the male inhabitants of such State, being twenty-one years of age, and citizens of the United States, or in any way abridged, except for participation in rebellion, or other crime, the basis of representation therein shall be reduced in the proportion which the number of such male citizens shall bear to the whole number of male citizens twenty-one years of age in such State.

SECTION 3

No person shall be a Senator or Representative in Congress, or elector of President and Vice President, or hold any office, civil or military, under the United States, or under any State, who, having previously taken an oath, as a member of Congress, or as an officer of the United States, or as a member of any State legislature, or as an executive or judicial officer of any State, to support the Constitution of the United States, shall have engaged in insurrection or rebellion against the same, or given aid or comfort to the enemies thereof. But Congress may by a vote of two-thirds of each House, remove such disability.

SECTION 4

The validity of the public debt of the United States, authorized by law, including debts incurred for payment of pensions and bounties for services in suppressing insurrection or rebellion, shall not be questioned. But neither the United States nor any State shall assume or pay any debt or obligation incurred in aid of insurrection or rebellion against the United States, or any claim for the loss or emancipation of any slave; but all such debts, obligations and claims shall be held illegal and void.

SECTION 5

The Congress shall have the power to enforce, by appropriate legislation, the provisions of this article.

AMENDMENT XV

Passed by Congress February 26, 1869; ratified February 3, 1870.

SECTION 1

The right of citizens of the United States to vote shall not be denied or abridged by the United States or by any State on account of race, color, or previous condition of servitude.

SECTION 2

The Congress shall have the power to enforce this article by appropriate legislation.

AMENDMENT XVI

Passed by Congress July 2, 1909; ratified February 3, 1913.

The Congress shall have power to lay and collect taxes on incomes, from whatever source derived, without apportionment among the several States, and without regard to any census or enumeration.

AMENDMENT XVII

Passed by Congress May 13, 1912; ratified April 8, 1913.

The Senate of the United States shall be composed of two Senators from each State, elected by the people thereof, for six years; and each Senator shall have one vote. The electors in each State shall have the qualifications requisite for electors of the most numerous branch of the State legislature.

When vacancies happen in the representation of any State in the Senate, the executive authority of such State shall issue writs of election to fill such vacancies: Provided, That the legislature of any State may empower the executive thereof to make temporary appointments until the people fill the vacancies by election as the legislature may direct.

This amendment shall not be so construed as to affect the election or term of any Senator chosen before it becomes valid as part of the Constitution.

AMENDMENT XVIII

Passed by Congress December 18, 1917; ratified January 16, 1919.

SECTION 1

After one year from the ratification of this article the manufacture, sale, or transportation of intoxicating liquors within, the importation thereof into, or the exportation thereof from the United States and all territory subject to the jurisdiction thereof for beverage purposes is hereby prohibited.

SECTION 2

The Congress and the several States shall have concurrent power to enforce this article by appropriate legislation.

SECTION 3

This article shall be inoperative unless it shall have been ratified as an amendment to the Constitution by the legislatures of the several States, as provided in the Constitution, within seven years from the date of the submission hereof to the States by the Congress.

AMENDMENT XIX

Passed by Congress June 4, 1919; ratified August 18, 1920.

The right of citizens of the United States to vote shall not be denied or abridged by the United States or by any State on account of sex. Congress shall have power to enforce this article by appropriate legislation.

AMENDMENT XX

Passed by Congress March 2, 1932; ratified January 23, 1933.

SECTION 1

The terms of the President and the Vice President shall end at noon on the 20th day of January, and the terms of Senators and Representatives at noon on the 3d day of January, of the years in which such terms would have ended if this article had not been ratified; and the terms of their successors shall then begin.

SECTION 2

The Congress shall assemble at least once in every year, and such meeting shall begin at noon on the 3d day of January, unless they shall by law appoint a different day.

SECTION 3

If, at the time fixed for the beginning of the term of the President, the President elect shall have died, the Vice President elect shall become President. If a President shall not have been chosen before the time fixed for the beginning of his term, or if the President elect shall have failed to qualify, then the Vice President elect shall act as President until a President shall have qualified;

and the Congress may by law provide for the case wherein neither a President elect nor a Vice President shall have qualified, declaring who shall then act as President, or the manner in which one who is to act shall be selected, and such person shall act accordingly until a President or Vice President shall have qualified.

SECTION 4

The Congress may by law provide for the case of the death of any of the persons from whom the House of Representatives may choose a President whenever the right of choice shall have devolved upon them, and for the case of the death of any of the persons from whom the Senate may choose a Vice President whenever the right of choice shall have devolved upon them.

SECTION 5

Sections 1 and 2 shall take effect on the 15th day of October following the ratification of this article.

SECTION 6

This article shall be inoperative unless it shall have been ratified as an amendment to the Constitution by the legislatures of three-fourths of the several States within seven years from the date of its submission.

AMENDMENT XXI

Passed by Congress February 20, 1933; ratified December 5, 1933.

SECTION 1

The eighteenth article of amendment to the Constitution of the United States is hereby repealed.

SECTION 2

The transportation or importation into any State, Territory, or possession of the United States for delivery or use therein of intoxicating liquors, in violation of the laws thereof, is hereby prohibited.

SECTION 3

This article shall be inoperative unless it shall have been ratified as an amendment to the Constitution by conventions in the several States, as provided in the Constitution, within seven years from the date of the submission hereof to the States by the Congress.

AMENDMENT XXII

Passed by Congress March 21, 1947; ratified February 27, 1951.

SECTION 1

No person shall be elected to the office of the President more than twice, and no person who has held the office of President, or acted as President, for more than two years of a term to which some other person was elected President shall be elected to the office of President more than once. But this Article shall not apply to any person holding the office of President when this Article was proposed by Congress, and shall not prevent any person who may be holding the office of President, or acting as President, during the term within which this Article becomes operative from holding the office of President or acting as President during the remainder of such term.

SECTION 2

This article shall be inoperative unless it shall have been ratified as an amendment to the Constitution by the legislatures of three-fourths of the several States within seven years from the date of its submission to the States by the Congress.

AMEND.MENT XXIII

Passed by Congress June 16, 1960; ratified March 29, 1961.

SECTION 1

The District constituting the seat of Government of the United States shall appoint in such manner as Congress may direct:

A number of electors of President and Vice President equal to the whole number of Senators and Representatives in Congress to which the District would be entitled if it were a State, but in no event more than the least populous State; they shall be in addition to those appointed by the States, but they shall be considered, for the purposes of the election of President and Vice President, to be electors appointed by a State; and they shall meet in the District and perform such duties as provided by the twelfth article of amendment.

SECTION 2

The Congress shall have power to enforce this article by appropriate legislation.

AMENDMENT XXIV

Passed by Congress August 27, 1962; ratified January 23, 1964.

SECTION 1

The right of citizens of the United States to vote in any primary or other election for President or Vice President, for electors for President or Vice President, or for Senator or Representative in Congress, shall not be denied or abridged by the United States or any State by reason of failure to pay poll tax or other tax.

SECTION 2

The Congress shall have power to enforce this article by appropriate legislation.

AMENDMENT XXV

Passed by Congress July 6, 1965; ratified February 10, 1967.

SECTION 1

In case of the removal of the President from office or of his death or resignation, the Vice President shall become President.

SECTION 2

Whenever there is a vacancy in the office of the Vice President the President shall nominate a Vice President who shall take office upon confirmation by a majority vote of both Houses of Congress.

SECTION 3

Whenever the President transmits to the President pro tempore of the Senate and the Speaker of the House of Representatives his written declaration that he is unable to discharge the powers and duties of his office, and until he transmits to them a written declaration to the contrary, such powers and duties shall be discharged by the Vice President as Acting President.

SECTION 4

Whenever the Vice President and a majority of either the principal officers of the executive departments or of such other body as Congress may by law provide, transmit to the President pro tempore of the Senate and the Speaker of the House of Representatives their written declaration that the President is unable to discharge the powers and duties of his office, the Vice President shall immediately assume the powers and duties of the office as Acting President.

Thereafter, when the President transmits to the President pro tempore of the Senate and the Speaker of the House of Representatives his written declaration that no inability exists, he shall resume the powers and duties of his office unless the Vice President and a majority of either the principal officers of the executive department or of such other body as Congress may by law provide, transmit within four days to the President pro tempore of the Senate and the Speaker of the House of Representatives their written declaration that the President is unable to discharge the powers and duties of his office. Thereupon Congress shall decide the issue, assembling within forty-eight hours for that purpose if not in session. If the Congress, within twenty-one days after receipt of the latter written declaration, or, if Congress is not in session, within twenty-one days after Congress is required to assemble, determines by two-thirds vote of both Houses that the President is unable to discharge the powers and duties of his office, the Vice President shall continue to discharge the same as Acting President; otherwise, the President shall resume the powers and duties of his office.

AMENDMENT XXVI

Passed by Congress March 23, 1971; ratified July 1, 1971.

SECTION 1

The right of citizens of the United States, who are eighteen years of age or older, to vote shall not be denied or abridged by the United States or by any State on account of age.

SECTION 2

The Congress shall have power to enforce this article by appropriate legislation.

AMENDMENT XXVII

Originally proposed Sept. 25, 1789; ratified May 7, 1992.

No law, varying the compensation for the services of the Senators and Representatives, shall take effect, until an election of representatives shall have intervened.

ACKNOWLEDGMENTS

There were many people behind the scenes in the making of this book, from those unknown in the early history of the world to those who are also unknown but can be found in writing their thoughts on the Internet. Of course there are those who write the books that we all learn from, and I have certainly learned a great deal by reading many different points of view on this and related subjects. One cannot learn without reading and digesting from many different sources, and that is how the world learns and grows wiser.

This is a relatively short book, and I wrote it to get to the point quickly and get people involved in governance. However, the book is the culmination of my having digested many, many books that have been written throughout history covering, among other subjects, famous principals from the past. These individuals include Alexander the Great, Julius Caesar, kings of England, George Washington, James Madison, Alexander Hamilton, Benjamin Franklin, Abraham, Moses, Jesus Christ, and Mohammed among others. All of these famous leaders as well as many others in the past who are not mentioned here have been influential in the making of history and in shaping the world we live in today.

In particular, I would like to thank my wife, Anne, for her patience with me and for her reading the manuscript as it developed, along with providing many suggestions for change, which I accepted in most instances. I also want to thank my grown children, Frank Sisson III, Benjamin Sisson, Lucy Wilhelm and William Sisson, for their support and encouragement while I wrote this book. I would also like to thank those who have promoted the idea of this book about the US Constitution to others that may want to learn more. I also want to thank William B. Matteson for his review of the book from a major law firm attorney's point of view and his opinion to go forward with the publication. I do not want to forget David St. John, executive editor of Elderberry Press, for his reading of my draft and his encouragement for the success of the book. I also do not want to forget Ric Wolford of Douglas Photographic Imaging in Wichita, Kansas, for his part in creating the cover for the book.

I am also grateful to all of those who have and will purchase this book and hopefully gain knowledge that will help restore our country to the place our founders hoped it to be for all posterity and that well-known goal is a more perfect Union into the future with liberty and justice for all.

BIBLIOGRAPHY

Bastiat, Frederick. *The Law.* New York: SoHo Books, 2007.

Conners, Shawn. *Know Your Government in 20 Minutes or Less: The Declaration of Independence, the U.S. Constitution and All Amendments.* 2012.

Federalist Papers Press, *The Original Federalist Case for the Constitution, 2009.*

Filmer, Robert. *Patriarcha and Other Writings.* Cambridge, UK: Cambridge University Press, 1991.

Gutzman, Kevin C. *James Madison and the Making of America.* New York: St. Martin's Press, 2012.

Hobbes, Thomas. *Leviathan.* England: 1680.

Locke, John. *Second Treatise of Government.* Feather Trail Press, 2009.

McClanahan, Brion. *The Founding Fathers Guide to the Constitution.* Washington, DC: Regnery Publishing, Inc. 2012.

Paine, Thomas. *Common Sense.* 1776.